KED
IN
XILE

NAKED IN EXILE

Khalil Hawi's *Threshing Floors of Hunger*

With Interpretation and Translation by Adnan Haydar and Michael Beard

An Original by Three Continents Press

First Edition

Three Continents Press
1346 Connecticut Avenue NW
Washington, DC 20036

ISBN: 0-89410-366-0
ISBN: 0-89410-367-9 (pbk)
LC No: 82-40406

The portrait sketch of Hawi is by Felicity Watts

Cover art by Kamal Boullata

In memoriam

Khalil Hawi
(1925–1982)

Acknowledgments

It is our pleasure to acknowledge, with great thanks, a generous grant from the Attiyeh Foundation of Washington, D.C. and Bismarck, North Dakota, a grant which in many ways made this book possible. We would also like to thank Mr. Abbas Bafakih and the University of North Dakota, both of whom made generous donations which helped us at crucial moments in the creation of this book.

Our translation and discussion of "The Cave" first appeared, in a slightly different form, in *Edebiyat: A Journal of Middle Eastern Literatures*. We would like to thank the editors of *Edebiyat* for permission to reprint them here. Special thanks go to Professors Sami Hawi and Iliya Hawi for granting us permission to reprint *Bayadir al-ju* in its Arabic original. We used the first edition (Beirut: Dar al-Adab, March, 1965) which can also be found, unchanged, in *Diwan Khalil Hawi* (Beirut: Dar al-Awda, July, 1972).

Dedication

As this book deals with the most reflexive of poets, we take the liberty of following suit and dedicating it to its own subject.

Preface

This book grew out of a series of conversations between the authors in 1978 and 1979, when Michael Beard was a Mellon Fellow at the University of Pennsylvania and Adnan Haydar was among his hosts at that institution, an environment where real dialogue between scholars from different backgrounds seems to take place more often than the laws of academic entropy would normally allow. The subject was frequently modern Arabic poetry, and a recurring leitmotif was the fact that Khalil Hawi has never received the attention abroad that we felt would be appropriate for a poet of his stature.

Hawi's suicide in June, 1982, increased our sense of urgency in this project. It intensified our conviction that to make Arabic poetry more accessible to western readers was more than an academic imperative. After each poem we have included an extensive interpretation designed to make Hawi's poetry more available both to those with a prior interest in modern Arabic literature and to the uninitiated general reader. The bibliography which follows may address the specialist more particularly, but we hope that our essays will make it more accessible to both readerships.

The previously unpublished poem "Ya sabiyya" located on pages 189-193—written in Hawi's hand on 14 April 1981— is one of Hawi's last poems. It can be taken as a summary of what we have demonstrated at length in the body of this book. It is not hard to find personal statements in Hawi's work when we know how to find them, but this one is peculiarly direct, at once a lyric moment and a microcosm of Hawian themes. The repeated Hawian terms *ramad* (ashes), *saqi'* (frost), *jamr* (ember), *tariy* (mellow), and *ghussa* (choking, agony, distress) as well as Hawian themes such as the constant pressing beyond boundaries (compare the opening of "Lazarus 1962") remind us of the consistency of his imagination.

It is at once a poem in the shape of a sexual experience and a history of Hawi's poetry. The scenario of an esthetic moment, which overshadows a life of experience suffused with bitterness and pain, with the ambiguity of context (which makes it problematic on whichever level the solution has taken place) is like a concentration of the Hawian carbon cycle. His oeuvre is a "body" of poetry in more than the traditional sense. As Emerson says of Montaigne: "cut these words and they would bleed."

ألعار يفضح كهفيَ ٱلمطويُّ

في منفى ٱلكهوفِ

وهل أصيح بمن يرجِّي ٱلمعجزاتْ

Shame strips my folded cave
Naked in its exile;
And shall I call for one
Who may work wonders yet?

NAKED IN EXILE

An Introduction

Khalil Hawi committed suicide when the Israeli Army first crossed the border into Lebanon, on 6 June 1982. It has only recently become possible to piece together the events of his last hours, and from what we can gather they seem characteristic of the Khalil Hawi we know from his poetry. The same evening he committed suicide he visited a friend, the poet Shafiq 'Ataya, who recalls Hawi quoting extensively from his own poem, "Lazarus 1962." Hawi spoke repeatedly of al-dhull (the shame) and al-'ar (the degradation) which he felt at the time, of his revulsion at the experience of seeing his country invaded. 'Ataya read Hawi one of his own poems, "Death of a Poet" (in English), which concludes "Life only shall begin/where life and death are one." Hawi commented, "You wrote that poem about me, didn't you?" 'Ataya replied that, no, he meant poets in general, that it was a poem about the nature of poetry. Hawi's cryptic reply was, "It's as if you were living in my heart."

His death was one of very many civilian casualties which accompanied that military operation. If we single him out, it is because his life work supplies a voice for the many thousand silent victims, though there is an elegance and indirection in that voice that may disguise to what extent he was concerned, devoted, even captivated by love for his country and for the people and the culture he did so much to enrich.

Hawi was a quiet, reclusive individual, unmarried and solitary. He could be expansive and open with students but

never at the expense of his personal privacy. Despite that characteristic privacy, his was a political death. There are people whose reaction to violence is relief that it has not happened to them, or self-righteous anger that it has happened at all and thus confirmed their pessimism. Hawi's death is a phenomenon of a different order altogether, that of a thinker who wanted nothing better than an opportunity to abandon his own pessimism (and who sometimes, as in his poem "The Wounded Thunder," succeeded), who was so totally unequipped with the defenses most of us put into play at the sight of suffering in others that he simply found himself unable to witness such suffering again.

We have suggested that his project as a poet was to speak for his people and his culture; we want to suggest also that "his people" is not confined to the Greek Orthodox community into which he was born, or to Lebanon, or even to the Arab world. His familiarity with western culture makes him one of the most accessible Arab poets to western readers. It would be hard to reflect Arab experience (Lebanese experience particularly) without acknowledging that East and West are rapidly ceasing to be separate categories.

Al-Shweir, the isolated mountain village in Lebanon where Khalil Hawi was born on New Year's Day, 1925,* was not so isolated as to separate him from early exposure to the world below. The Ottoman Empire which had ended with the Great War was very much in public consciousness, and contact with the West was more tangible still. He began to attend the local French missionary schools at the age of five, becoming familiar not only with the direct influence of western education, but the influence of western political thinkers. Al-Shweir is tucked in the valley below Dhur Al-Shweir, a village made famous by the presence of Antun Sa'ada, founder in the early 1930s of the influential Parti Populaire Syrien (*Al-Hizb al-suri al-qawmi*), an early and powerful influence on Hawi's social vision.

His family was not wealthy. At fourteen, in fact, he was forced to interrupt his secondary education and work as a wall-plasterer and bricklayer in the (now occupied) Golan Heights. Such jobs were seasonal (from March to November), leaving him winters to supplement his education; he recalls during this period reading, in French, the poetry of Lamartine, de Vigny, de Musset, Baudelaire, Verlaine and Valéry. Among English poets he admired Blake, Coleridge and Shelley.

---

*There is doubt about the year. Some informants suggest 1919 as his date of birth, though available printed sources all agree on 1925.

Sources of his enthusiasm from the classical Arabic tradition were Jarir and Al-Mutanabbi; Kahlil Gibran was a more specific visible influence. Hawi's first poems, perhaps with Gibran's colloquial poetry as a model, were in the Lebanese dialect, though the writing through which he came to public attention was in standard literary Arabic. This was through a poem he wrote in 1947, while a freshman at the American University of Beirut; he entered it in a poetry contest sponsored by the members of a political society, "Al-'Urwa al-Wuthqa" ("The Tie that binds"). The poem, entitled "A God," attracted considerable attention in the society's magazine.

Though as an undergraduate he was a serious student, supported by a scholarship which required exceptional grades, most of his reminiscences of his undergraduate days are political in nature. (The events of 1948 made politics and daily life converge.) The political teachings of Antun Sa'ada and Constantine Zurayq (a political theorist of Arab nationalism who taught history at A.U.B.) must have seemed to descend suddenly out of the realm of theory altogether. During this period Antun Sa'ada was living in Beirut, across from the American University campus, and Hawi was a member of his Parti Populaire Syrien, at least temporarily. Eventually he disclaimed all affiliation with individual parties, continuing to identify himself with Arab nationalist movements in general, but with the awareness that connection with any one party might restrict him as a writer.

If we did not know how his life ended, it would be easy to see it as an unalloyed success story, a career of repeated triumphs. He graduated in 1950 with a B.A. in Arabic literature (with a strong background in European literature and philosophy). In 1951 he was appointed a lecturer in the Department of Arabic at A.U.B. A primary goal of this period was paying back the debts he had incurred during his undergraduate years, but despite full-time teaching and additional tutoring he managed in 1952 to complete a much commented-upon M.A. thesis, "Faith and Reason Between al-Ghazzali and Averroes." He continued to teach at the A.U.B. Arabic Department until 1956, when he went to Cambridge University for his doctorate. The first poem in his fully recognizable voice "The Mariner and The Dervish," was published shortly before his departure, the Mariner being the first of his allegorical heroes, who continue to appear in his *diwans* in various incarnations, informing an ever more complex vision of philosophy, esthetics and history.

To judge from references in his writing, Hawi was not fond of university life at Cambridge. A poem from this period, later collected in "The Wind and the Flute" (*Al-Nay wa al-rih*, 1960), includes a specific separation of his own sensibility and that in which he found himself:

> Between me and the door are pencils
> inkwells
> a shy echo
> piles of yellowing paper
> . . .
> I'm not one of you
> progeny of monks
> and dry meat
> of the monastery.
> My blood will not revert
>   to its component chemicals
> I lied   I lied
> drag me to the courtyard
> strip me naked
> peel off the insignia
>   of the university.

There were presumably ameliorating factors; his studies with F. R. Leavis altered considerably the attitude towards romanticism in his poems. His doctoral dissertation, *Kahlil Gibran: His Background, Character and Works*, was supervised by the prominent Orientalist A. J. Arberry, who was so impressed with it that he invited Hawi to collaborate with him in a survey of modern Arabic literature. The survey failed to materialize: instead Hawi accepted an assistant professorship at the American University of Beirut, where he taught until the end of his life.

The poetry from his Cambridge period culminates in the collection "The River of Ashes" (*Nahr al-ramad*, 1957), followed by "The Wind and the Flute" (*Al-Nay wa al-rih*, 1961),

which won him the prize for that year from the Lebanese
literary society, "Friends of the Book."* The volume we have
translated, *The Threshing Floors of Hunger* (*Bayadir al-ju'*,
1965), occupies, it seems to us, a summational position in
Hawi's oeuvre. Not only do themes which have evolved in the
early collections come full term here, but after this work there
is a long period of silence, broken abruptly and authoritatively
by the appearance of "The Wounded Thunder" (*Al-Ra'd al-
jarih*, 1979) and "From Comedy's Inferno" (*Min Jahim al-
kumidya*, 1979), a thirteen year period during which we have
from him only occasional poems. Of the three poems which
make up *The Threshing Floors of Hunger* the first two, "The
Cave" and "The Genie of the Beach" are relatively more
accessible to western readers. Neither are simple poems, but
both have a self-contained quality, a confined lexicon of
imagery, which makes them more nearly universal statements
about the nature of the imagination and its limits. "The Cave"
(1962) centers on a direct objectification of a mood into
landscape imagery; "The Genie of the Beach" (1962) (which
will be more comprehensible after we are familiar with
"Lazarus, 1962" because it offers an inward-turning
protagonist, a variation of Hawi's savior heroes, of whom
more momentarily) presents us with dizzying shifts of setting
and character, but within a scope of reference (oppositions of
urban versus nomadic life, of beach versus mountain) which
is not limited to the cultural experience of Arab readers only.
"Lazarus 1962," however, the focal poem of the collection, is
a reading of a specific moment of history in which the first
wave of Arab revolutions in the twentieth century as well as
the Mongol invasions of the thirteenth are filtered through the
story of Lazarus. At the same time, it refers outward to
Hawi's earlier poems, to the series of savior figures, culture-
heroes who would be valid for the contemporary Arab world.
The sailor of "The Mariner and the Dervish" and Sindbad of
"Sindbad's Eighth Voyage" are the primary examples,
Odysseus figures updated and adapted to the non-western
world. Hawi's Lazarus is the fullest depiction of such a
character, and by far the most negative, so much so that

---

*"The Wind and the Flute" is to appear shortly in an English version by
Lewis Ware published by Albany Press, Emeryville, California.

"Lazarus, 1962" foreshadows an entire decade of Arab writing, in which the disillusionment which followed the 1967 war produced a rich tradition of waste-land writing.

The creation of an archetypal Arab hero, even of a series of such heroes, does not in itself sum up Hawi's contribution as a poet. It may be more accurate to consider those heroes, with their sudden metamorphoses and simultaneous levels of identity, as a framework around which he has been able to develop two farther innovations. First we notice Hawi's idiosyncratic style: those constantly shifting landscapes in which multiple figurative levels evolve on two or three fronts simultaneously, allowing him to exploit with startling efficiency the (also startling) evocative resources of the Arabic language. The second innovation may strike us as paradoxical, that the surrealistic surface of Hawi's poetry is such an effective vehicle for political vision. But since the content of the political vision of "Lazarus, 1962" is a message of illusion versus realities, of paradox and ambiguity, it is perhaps articulated more directly in poetry than in paraphrase. Hawi's Lazarus is no simple representation of tyranny or corruption, but at once an embodiment of the *manaqib* or *virtù* which an anti-colonial society requires and also a fundamental derailment of that power, a process by which he comes to resemble the forces he has opposed. If we were to sum up the characteristics of the "Hawian" hero in his manifestation as Lazarus, the most nearly accurate word might be specularity, an uncanny confrontation of opposites as mirror images which recurs in fact throughout *The Threshing Floors of Hunger*.

"The Wounded Thunder," the poem whose hero in a sense revises that of "Lazarus, 1962" thirteen years later, is a hopeful, perhaps even a celebratory statement. In retrospect we may see it as a commentary on the new mood of the Arab world, evolving since the 1973 war, a committed resignation to permanent resistance, a kind of Fanonian existentialism, which has gradually been replacing the naive trust in providence of previous generations, but it would be wrong to make Hawi's philosophy so programmatic or predictable: in the prose introduction to that poem he observes that he was himself surprised to see the poem take this form. This ability to surprise himself Hawi shares with many accomplished poets but the ability to share that sense of discovery with the reader, without compromising the integrity of the work is more rare. We argued above for the privileged position of *The Threshing Floors of Hunger* among Hawi's writings, but we should not let that statement pass without our own revision: ideally our understanding of Hawi should take in the unfolding of his works from "The Mariner and the Dervish" at least. It is as if Hawi were a poet with a single vision whose power is its adaptability, a poet who tests and questions that vision repeatedly. This is one reason why the Hawian vocabulary of key terms—*mu'anat, ru'ya, ramad* (experience, vision, ashes)—charged with personal significance which carries over from one work to the next, is so useful to him, and so appropriate to his particular mode of creation. (His "restricted" vocabulary is, strangely, considered a defect by some critics.)

"From Comedy's Inferno," published a month after "The Wounded Thunder," part of the same wave of creation that broke Hawi's thirteen-year silence, exemplifies this mode of coherence even more plainly. Most of its poems are short and lyrical, fraught with formal experiments in the untapped rhythmical possibilities of classical Arabic meters. The subject matter is new, but it is still held together by a network of allusions to Hawi's previous writings and stamped with the signature of his personalized vocabulary.

Like the concept of the archetypal hero, the lexicon of readily identifiable Hawian terms acts as a stable point of reference around which his sudden, shifting flights of thought and imagery can be effectively set off, giving his work a visionary fictionality.

There are many kinds of integrity, two particularly which seem appropriate to the artist in the modern world. One is a constant responsiveness to the new, an aspiration towards contemporaneity which sets out to track down conventionality and explode it, to remake language, to rename and redefine. This typifies Arab modernist experiments. Another kind of integrity works from inside the tradition outwards, an esthetic of reworking in which each new creation is designed to echo a consistent body of personal tradition, to open it for further development, growth and expansion. This is Hawi's integrity, a lonelier path perhaps, but we suspect that the nature of his death verifies how intimately the private poet experienced the public life of his people.

The Cave

وعرفتُ كيف تمطُّ أرجلها ٱلدقائقُ

كيف تجمد ، تستحيل إلى عصورْ

وغدوتُ كهفاً في كهوف ٱلشطِّ

يدمع جبهتي

ليلُ تحجَّر في ٱلصخورْ

وتركتُ خيل ٱلبحر تعلكُ

لحم أحشائي

تغيّبه بصحراءِ ٱلمدى

عاينتُ رعب زوارقٍ

تهوي مكسَّرة ٱلصدى ،

عبثاً يدوِّي عبر أقبيتي ٱلصدى

يلقي على عينيَّ ليل جدائلٍ

في ٱلريح تُعولُ ، تستغيثُ ، وترتمي

The Cave

And I have come to know how minutes drag their feet
And how they petrify, metamorphose into centuries.
And I've become a cave among the caves on shore;
A night that calloused in the rocks has blotched my brow.
And I have suffered Neptune's steeds to chew the flesh   5
Of my entrails and lose it in the desert of the deep.
I have observed the dread of ships falling headlong
In broken echoes that wail in vain into my depths
And cast upon my eyes a night of flowing locks
Howling into the wind, entreating, falling helplessly.   10

غبَّ آنسحاب آلبحرِ

يرسب في دمي

سمك مواتْ ،

بعض أثمار معفنة ، قشورْ

ويدي تميع وتنطوي في آلرملِ ،

ريحُ آلرمل تنخرها ،

وتصفر في آلعروقْ

ويحزُّ في جسدي وما يدميهِ

سكّين عتيقْ ،

لو كان لي عصبٌ يثورْ

ربَّاهُ كيف تمطُّ أرجلَها آلدقائقُ

كيف تجمدُ ، تستحيلُ إلى عصورْ

With the retreating sea there settle in my blood
Dead fish, some rotten fruit, some peels; and in the sand
My hand caves in; it folds and carious grows;
The sand-wind riddles through and whistles in its veins.
An old and rusty dagger cuts into my flesh   15
And leaves a deep impression, but I do not bleed.
Had I but one rebellious vein!
Dear God, how ruthlessly the minutes drag their feet
And how they petrify, metamorphose into centuries.

يا من حللتَ وكنتَ لي

ضيفاً على غيرِ ٱنتظارْ

وملأتَ مائدتي

بطيب ٱلمنّ وٱلسلوى

سكبتَ ٱلخمر مما ليس تعرفهُ ٱلجرار

أعطيتني مُلكاً على جنّ ٱلمغاور وٱلبحار

ما يشتهي قلبي تجسّده يدي

في ٱلطين يخفقُ ما تغيّبه ٱلظنون :

حورٌ ، يواقيتٌ ، عماراتٌ

بضربةِ ساحرٍ .: « كوني تكونْ »

ألنارُ تزهرُ ملء موقدتي

وتثمرُ ، وٱلربيعْ

يحبو ويفرش غرفتي

غبّ ٱلصقيعْ

Behold! Thou hast prevailed,   20
An unawaited guest,
Lavished the choicest quail
And manna on my board,
Hast waited on my cup
With wine unknown to jars,   25
Empowered me to rule
The genie of the caves,
Thou hast imbued my hands
With might to mould my dreams,
Enlivened in the clay   30
What hopes cannot perceive.
Behold! Now nymphs, now gems,
Now lofty palaces;
The wizard strikes his wand:
"Let there be," and there is.   35
The fire flowers, ripens
On my hearth, and spring
Tiptoes and canopies
My room amid the frost;

والشمسُ تأوي من ضبابِ ٱلقُطْبِ

أُدفئها ، وتمضي مطمئنّةً

أني بغيبتها أحرُّ ٱلجمرةَ ٱلخضراءَ

وأخصبُ أرضنا من غيرِ مِنّةْ

.

يا من حملت إليَّ طِيبَ ٱلمنِّ وٱلسلوى

بسطتَ يدي على جنٍّ

تجسَّد ما أُريدْ

وخجلتُ من فقري ،

سفحتُ دمي ، ذبحتُ لك ٱلوريد

لا تحتجبْ بمغاورِ ٱلأُفقِ

ٱلمجمَّر وٱلمصفَّحِ بٱلحديدْ ،

عينايَ سمَّرتا على أُفقِ

ٱلحديدِ بلا جفونْ

The sun, returning home,   40
Dispels the polar fog
And, basking in my warmth,
Contented, passes on.
Awaiting its return,
I stir the green ember   45
And fructify our land
With bounty, effortless.

Thou that hast favoured me
With manna and with quail,
Empowered me to rule   50
The genie of the caves,
Imbued my hands with might
To mold and to create,
I have become ashamed
Of my own poverty.   55
For thee I spilled my blood,
Butchered the only vein
In reverential fear
And due expectancy.
Hide not in leaden caves   60
Out of the range of sight;
My eyes are lidless, nailed
To curtained horizons.

وأخاف منِ كبريت صاعقةٍ

يفجّر فيها ضَحكَ ٱلجنونْ

ما عدتُ أعرف مَنْ تكون ،

أللعنةُ ٱلحمراءُ في شفتي

وفي شفتي ٱلتوجع وٱلصلاةْ ،

ألعار يفضح كهيَ ٱلمطويُّ

في منفى ٱلكهوفِ

وهل أصيح بمن يربّجي ٱلمعجزاتْ

ألساحرُ ٱلجبار كان هنا وماتْ ؟

مِن جثة ٱلجبارِ

كيف تبخّرتْ خِرَقْ ،

وكيف تكوّرتْ شبحاً غريبْ

يمضي وتنفضه ٱلدروبُ إلى ٱلدروبْ .

And now I'm horrified
Of the sulphurous blaze   65
Of sudden thunderbolt
That blasts into my eyes
Peals of insanity.
I know not who you are.
Damnation rages red   70
Upon my lips and pain
And prayer leave their brand
Upon them and contend.
Shame strips my folded cave
Naked in its exile;   75
And shall I call for one
Who may work wonders yet?
The great magician died
And he will not return.
From the magician's corpse   80
A tattered rag somehow
Evaporates. It grows:
Some sprightly form sets forth
Unfurled and chased along
From road to wayward road.   85

أُمَّاهُ لا تسترحمي

بِالدمع في غَبش العَشيةِ ، لن أُجيبْ :

« خلف الكهوفِ ، وخلف صحراء الشواطىء »

« معولٌ ، حقلٌ ، ومكتبةٌ ودارْ »

ـ ملكي على جن المغاور والبحار !

ألمنُّ والسلوى

وخمرٌ ليس تعرفُها الجِرار !

ماذا سوى كهفٍ يجوع ، فمٍ يبورْ

ويدٍ مجوَّفةٍ تخطُّ وتمسحُ

الخطَّ المجوَّفَ في فتورْ ؟

هذي العقاربُ لا تدورْ ،

ربَّاهُ كيف تمطُّ أرجلَها الدقائقْ

كيف تجمدُ ، تستحيل إلى عصورْ !

When evening haze prevails
Save your maternal tears;
Entreat me not to say:
"Behind the wasted caves
Behind the barren shores   90
A world of books, a home
A field, a plough, await."
My kingdom is not there.
Omnipotent I rule
The genie of the caves.   95
Manna and quail and wine
Unknown to earthly jars.
What but a hungry cave, a wasted yawning mouth,
A hollow hand that drags and draws the hollow line
Only to wipe it out with slow tepidity?   100
The tedious clock is stopped; its hands are frozen still.
And O! how ruthlessly the minutes drag their feet
And how they petrify, metamorphose into centuries.

Two Interpretations of Khalil Hawi's
"The Cave"

Every translation is an interpretation, no matter how literal it
may attempt to be. This translation is not a literal one
attempting to evade the inevitability of interpreting the text.
It may be literal if by that we mean that it renders the ex-
perience of the poem on as many levels of significance as
possible. Over the course of extensive discussions of this
translation the authors became increasingly conscious
of a specific reading of the poem traced by the negative shape
between the English and Arabic texts. We offer them both,
translation and synoptic analysis, as companion readings
mutually dependent.

The untranslatable elements were our first concern: the
allusiveness of Hawi's Koranic and Biblical diction in Arabic,
for instance, seemed transferable into English only through an
occasional archaism. Allusion was the most pervasive
problem: an English "al-Kahf" will never have the same past as
its prototype; it will never be rooted outside of itself in the
same network of specific usages in Arabic poetry and
prophetic language. Likewise Arabic quantitative rhythm
inevitably falls into the category of the untranslatable, but we
feel that the varied combination of iambic feet in the English
version (between three and seven) suggest the monometric
effect of the original. Hawi uses the foot of the *kamil* meter
(uu—u—) in groups of from one to three, occasionally splitting

the foot and continuing it in the following line, the determining factor being the poetic sentence. The translation uses enjambment to suggest an effect similar to that of splitting of poetic feet. We cannot refute George Steiner's observation on the inflationary nature of poetry,[1] since our translation confronts the 78 lines of "al-Kahf" with 103. Our line references are to the English translation. We trust that the curious reader will be able to locate individual passages in the Arabic text. The division into three parts is that of the original.

The poem's difficulty resides not in the problem of finding meaning but in the multiplicity of possible meanings, which blur the distinction between literal readings—which shift repeatedly—and the reader's sense of a perhaps vague coherent shape. Example: the image of the cave has so many possible references in European and Islamic traditions that it can hardly be said to have a unified significance. In Plato's cave (which is common to both Middle Eastern and European traditions) it represents the created world. In a Freudian scheme it stands for a particular part of the body. In the stories of the Prophet Mohammad it is the scene of inspiration; in the Koran it is the place where the seven sleepers of Ephesus take refuge from persecution. Caves are common places of refuge for Old Testament prophets: David in I Samuel 24.3, Elijah in I Kings 19.9. In the Gospels a cave is the scene of the Resurrection. In mystical interpretations of the story of Joseph, Joseph in the pit (bi'r, "the well") expresses something like mankind in Plato's cave. The numerous fragmentary critical pronouncements about this poem have concentrated on wider contexts: Arab society and the corpus of Hawi's works. Muta' Safadi, for example, sees it as a link in the evolution of Hawi's attitudes toward the social and political decadence of modern Arab civilization, a re-capitulation of the theme of futility that he finds expressed in "Sindbad in his Eighth Journey," the last poem of "The Wind and the Flute."[2] Hani al-Rahib argues against the pessimistic interpretation of "Sindbad" and finds that poem at variance with the mood of "The Cave."[3] Another point of disagreement is the question of the persona's attachment to the cave, although both critics agree that the cave is a symbol of stagnation and sterility. Their positions, we feel, are weakened

by premature foregrounding of political and social
dimensions: the poet attempting to return to the roots of his
civilization, as Safadi contends, and the poet's rejection of
those roots, as Al-Rahib interprets. Mustafa Badawi sees a
continuum between "The River of Ashes," Hawi's first divan,
and "Al-Kahf" (1962), bypassing "The Wind and the Flute,"
which comes between. Following Safadi, Mustafa Badawi
reads the poem as an expression of "fruitless waiting that
borders on despair."[4] To our knowledge no analytical study
of the poem has yet been attempted.

The unmistakable connections between "The Cave" and
the rest of Hawi's corpus notwithstanding, it may be salutary
to start from the inside and work out. The peculiar feeling
established in the opening lines by the identification of self with
cave, of poet with landscape, of animate and inanimate
entities, evokes contradictory responses. There is a tradition
of poets wishing to partake in the properties of natural
objects—from Tamim ibn Muqbil's "Law anna-l-fata hajarun,"
which Adonis makes the keynote for an understanding of the
pre-Islamic sensibility,[5] to Prufrock's "I should have been a
pair of ragged claws"—which usually suggests an escape from
the ambiguities of life in society. The transformation in "The
Cave" is not something so straightforward as an escape from
the human condition; nor is it so simple as an exemplification
of a particular mood. If we respond to the image naively, the
tone is melancholy, but there is a muted exuberance in the
suddenness and gratuitousness of identification which
tempers that mood. We might call this a conflict of con-
tent and form, but the conflict persists even on the level
of content alone. Among the possible significances of
the word cave functioning visibly in Hawi's poem there
are at least two contradictory aspects: the cave as refuge,
a desired, protecting enclosure, and the cave as a prison,
a place of banishment, a sinister site of confinement some-
how opposed to poetic creation. In any event, solitude:
whether the solitude of the prophet awaiting divine in-
spiration (Muhammad in the cave of Hira') or, as Safadi
suggests, the individual withdrawn from public life in a
despotic society.

As the cave evades reduction into a particular univalent

symbol, the narrative motion of the poem similarly resists the
illusion of motion toward a goal, the inexorable unfolding of
meaning. The reader who looks for narrative development, a
story, will be betrayed at every bend of the road. The
polyvalent quality of the cave substitutes a narrative of a
different kind, where the cave as a symbol resists sequential
logic. The sequence of icons, or states, which inform the poem
are not causally bound. They are separated by gaps (the
temporal equivalent of caves?), which make the succession of
scenes less a development ("the cave's progress" or
"adventures of a cave") than a catalog of possibilities which
universalizes those scenes simply because they are not bound
by anticipated narrative cause and effect. In the course of
writing the synopsis which follows we felt a certain tug towards
narrative continuity, a tendency to fill in too many gaps, which
we tried to resist, perhaps imperfectly. Our synopsis starts
with the opening lines, themselves problematical because they
will function as a leitmotif in two other places in the poem (11.
18-19, 102-03).

The polyvalence of the cave is essential: a hungry mouth, a
sterile womb, a religious supplicant empty of faith, a sound
divested of meaning. The persona's commitment to the cave,
his refusal to leave it in spite of everything, is not commitment
to a specific ideal; the cave is not itself inspiration or
redemption. It is a commitment to banishment, exile
conceived as an intermediary to vision rather than the thing
itself.

The opening lines employ a device typical of Hawi, namely,
metaphors which accumulate, expand and cancel each other
out. His invocation of time first describes it as personified little
creatures, minutes which drag their feet: almost a cartoon
image. They take on a death-like rigor and finally
"metamorphose into centuries," become an endless spatial
extension, something that reaches beyond the individual's
range of vision. Simultaneously, we encounter a subtle
transference of that chain of metaphors in which the process
of solidification contaminates the speaker, moving across
from the third person (the solidifying minutes) to the first, from
observed to observer. The opening scene (lines one to ten)
contains four conspicuous first-person verbs ascribed to the
conscious will of the persona. The verb 'araftu ('arafa, "to

know"), which has clear present perfect implications, stretches his act of knowing into the past where it is solidified and no longer accessible, and leaves intact a possible tentative relation with a future repetition of the act. (Its relation to the past is metonymic: it touches; to the future, metaphorical: it works across a gap.) The object of his knowing is a metamorphosis, *tastahil* (*istahala*, "to metamorphose") but it is a metamorphosis which ends in stasis: time divested of the possibility of a future. At best then it is a knowledge which is devoid of promise. With the second verb, *ghadawtu* (*ghada*, "to become") the process of encroachment by which time first solidified then began to pass its stillness on, is complete, as if the object of his knowing, an act of solidification, had engulfed him. The aspectual property of *ghadawtu* has future implications, but a future which is checked, a future of stasis, "a night that calloused . . ." He has become a cave among the caves, etc., a night which stops short of metamorphosing into day. With *taraktu* (*taraka*, "to leave, allow, suffer") the ambiguity of active and passive coalesces; the ambiguity of a verb which is semantically passive but grammatically active parallels the paradox of taking the cave as an object: is the cave the solid rock which encloses emptiness, or is it emptiness itself? *Taraktu* in its dimension of helplessness becomes the logical action of the persona turned into a cave. The fourth verb is aspectually similar to the other verbs in bridging the past and present, but it differs in the degree of helplessness, which has been gradually augmented. Nor is this augmentation unanticipated, because lines 5 and 6 obliterate all the senses but that of sight, and empty the persona of all corporeal being. *'Ayantu* (*'ayana*, "to see") repeats *'araftu* ("to know") but in weakened form, and between the two is the decline from human to object. The process of losing identity in degrees is the ordering principle of these lines, each image marking a stage in it. The poet is reduced to a pair of eyes, but even sight, his last fading connection with the world of the senses, is blocked. He observes sinking ships and the same storm (in a Shelleyan image: see "Ode to the West Wind" ll. 18-24) darkens his vision.

In the scene which follows (ll. 11-19) the speaker's agency is absent altogether. Action contained in the verbs is performed without the speaker's volition. The mood is that of the calm after the storm, in which he takes stock of his own powerlessness. The focus is not on the aggressing sea but what it leaves behind, its refuse. The extraordinary simultaneity of being and non-being in his self-description focuses on his hands, which will re-emerge as a central image, still hollow, in the concluding scenes. The hand thrust into the sandy beach, a traditional emblem for attempting to grasp the ungraspable, becomes the image of a hand itself turned into sand, grown porous, crumbling, blending with the landscape, a passivity so total that the physical integrity of the self disappears. The speaker is penetrated, violated by waves, by wind, by rusty dagger, yet violation in this stanza is preempted by the speaker's own prior decay and dissolution. The demand for a rebellious vein is at this point a wish to feel, to experience the pain he can acknowledge only intellectually. The repetition of the opening couplet (ll. 18-19) elicits a simultaneous reaction: it conveys a sense of helplessness by breaking down our illusion of narrative progress but it also works as a reprise, a comforting, somehow lyrical or musical recapitulation of the theme of helplessness. Formal and semantic properties have parted.

The section comprising lines 20-35 reads as an almost programmatic reversal of the imagery in the opening two scenes. One is struck immediately by the utter lack of transition, the rhetorical abruptness with which images of decay and death are metamorphosed into their contrary. We might suppose ourselves in a different poem altogether except for the images which oppose elements from previous scenes: "manna" and "quail" answer the images of decayed food in the opening; the hand which molds in clay reverses the image of the porous, passive hand dissolved into the sand above (ll. 13-14). The speaker's altered situation is portrayed in a series of projections into various scenes from Biblical and Koranic narrative. At first he is in the role of the passive recipient of divine grace ("manna" and "quail") like the companions of Moses in Exodus or in the Koran (2.57, 7.160, 20.80). The drink he is served, "wine unknown to jars," suggests the miraculous wine in the first miracle of Jesus at Cana in Galilee, or the sacrament of transubstantiation generally, but also the spiritual wine referred to in Sufi poetry, also often described as untainted by earthly fabrication (*sakirna biha min qabli an*

yukhlaqa-l-karmu in Ibn al-Farid's *Mimiyya*). His power over
the genie of the cave (in a sense over his previous self, the
cave) represents an intermediary stage, represented perhaps
by the Solomon of the Koran (*Surat al-Naml*) or by the heroes
of numerous narratives in the *Thousand and One Nights*. In
the final stage he occupies the role of creator, kneading clay
and fashioning "what hopes cannot perceive," echoing the
words that open Genesis (or the Koran: 2.117, 16.40). His
sense of power has analogues in the accounts of mystics and
in the common equation of poetic and divine creation, but it is
clear that there is still a line of demarcation between him and
the wizard who briefly materializes in line 34. A disjunction
persists throughout this and the following section between the
speaker's sense of power and his grammatical role as object
rather than agent of the verbs' action.

The catalog of powers which climaxes in lines 46-47 is
summarized in the concluding phrase, its effortlessness: *min
ghayri minna*. Instead of his acting on things (either
semantically or grammatically), things, forces of nature,
heavenly powers, come to him. Instead of a cave, the setting is
a domestic scene, a room with a fireplace, which contrasts in
mood with the sinister opening landscape and in scale with the
celestial forces which bend to his will. It is as though the fire of
his hearth were the heat of creation, where the seasons unfold
and bend to his creative power.

To this point we have seen two antithetical states or stages
separated by the gap between lines 19 and 20. In the passages
that follow we will see the area between them. The scene
which begins with line 20 portrays a sheltered space or
moment when the powers of the ecstatic vision are cataloged
without reference to their temporary nature. It is an important
component of the experience of the poem that the highest
point of inspiration is described without anticipating its
transient nature. The qualities of the ecstatic moment are
expressed through the juxtaposition of two kinds of energy,
the intense concentrated energy of fire and the gradual energy
of growing things. The red and the green. Thus fire "ripens"
and the embers are the colors of leaves. The imagery is
reminiscent (purposely?) of Dylan Thomas' apocalyptic
moments: "the force that through the green fuse drives the
flower . . ." The pattern of metaphor moves simultaneously

outward (fire as sun, plants as the returning spring) and in-
ward: the cosmological scene unwinds in the fireplace
(*mawqidati*) of the persona's domestic enclosure (now
ghurfati, no longer cave). The tension that existed between
the persona and the forces of nature has now become
redemptive, enabling him for the time being not just to feel
at one with the forces of nature but to feel that his power
supplants them:

> The sun, returning home,
> Dispels the polar fog
> And, basking in my warmth,
> Contented, passes on.
> Awaiting its return,
> I stir the green ember
> And fructify our land
> With bounty, effortless.

With the scene beginning with line 48, where the ecstatic
vision fades and we begin to move downwards from a state of
plenitude to the original state of absence, we begin to
perceive an over-all, containing form that may be termed
musical. The movement is analogous to that of a common
western melody type, where an initial wide interval (here
analogous to ll. 1-19 versus 20-47) is filled by successive
melodic phrases (here analogous to ll. 48-103) or perhaps on
another level to the movement from a second theme back to
the restatement of a first theme. Line 48 ("*Ya man hamalta*")
echoes line 20 ("*Ya man halalta*") but with the substitution of
a more physical, common verb (*hamala*, "to carry, bring
over"/*halla*, "to manifest oneself to, to transfigure, to fill with
presence"). Although the speaker's powers described in lines
20-45 are passive, powers which work through him, initiated
by a higher agency, lines 45-47 reverse the picture, giving the
persona a momentarily active role in creation (*udfi'u-ha*, "I
warm it [the sun]"). At that point the distinction between the
higher force and the persona is leveled smooth. We are close
to the Rimbauldian notion of the poet as sorcerer, alchemist,
thaumaturge who takes on miraculous powers, capturing
them for his own profit. What distinguishes the persona of
line 48-79 (the fading vision) from that figure, however, is his
awareness of separation from the source of power, which

remains omnipotent and at a distance: "Hide not in leaden caves/out of the range of sight" (ll. 60-61).

Amid the bewildering tranformations of self there has remained one constant: an I-thou axis, a self who seeks, an "other" who bestows. The other, the one addressed, whether poetic muse or deity, is never defined in specific terms except through actions of giving ("*Ya man halalta*") but in the section of declining vision he is envisioned by the speaker as a replica of himself, another individual who hides in caves (ll. 60-61). The process is reminiscent of Lear in his madness, interpreting everything in terms of his own condition: "What, have his daughters brought him to this pass?" (*King Lear*, 3.4). Images of self proliferate so quickly that it becomes difficult to articulate them with a language of stable pronouns (as the authors discovered trying to write the following sentences). The magician figure, for example: is he an image of self or an incarnation of the bestowing thou? The bestowing thou: if it has retreated across the horizon into a cave like the persona's becoming in effect a mirror image of the persona, does this mean that the persona's "self" has always been in fact its own bestowing power, or does it mean that the concept of the bestowing power as a "self" is itself a symptom of declining vision? What is clear is that this uncanny relationship between two figures in facing caves underlines the speaker's despair in creative power itself. It is as if awareness of the speaker's identity as an individual was itself the process of falling from grace. In this light, *Wa khajaltu min faqri*, ("And I became ashamed of my own poverty," ll. 54-55), a phrase given particular prominence rhythmically by the unanticipated caesura which follows it, is an ironic reversal of the Sufi praise of poverty, Suhrawardi's *Al-faqru fakhri*, "Poverty is my pride."[6] In this stage inspiration has ceased to be a redemptive gift; it is seen as a threat, a thunderbolt, an image of prophecy but also of punishment. This consciousness reaches its climax at the verb *akhafu* (*khafa*, "to be frightened"), the apex of his self-awareness.

Heightened awareness of self evolves in line 69 into ignorance of the other ("I know not who you are"), and it is against the background of the mood of despair which colors this section that we see the core of the poem, the glimpse of

the contradictory process of creation in all its problematic
complexity.

> And shall I call for one
> Who may work wonders yet?
> The great magician died
> And He will not return.
> From the magician's corpse
> A tattered rag somehow
> Evaporates; It grows:
> Some sprightly form sets forth
> Unfurled and chased along
> From road to wayward road.

We read the magician figure as the speaker's self in the role of
poet, during the process of inspiration, a figure who can be
said to die when inspiration fades. There remain a dead body
and something that emerges from it: khiraq, "rags" but also a
kind of spirit. As spirit, it escapes. As rags (khirqa, particularly
the kind of patched cloak which traditionally characterizes the
Sufi), it suggests not only cloth and clothes but perhaps
a shroud, something extraneous but metonymically tied to the
figure of the dead magician. (Are clothes the man? Is the poem
the poet? Yes and no.) The images of the miraculous in the
description of creative powers (the lofty palaces, l.33, the
green embers, l.45) were indeed marvelous and moving, but
since we encountered them against a buoyant magical scene,
we accepted them as natural in their magical environment.
They were part of a "marvelous" world in Todorov's terms.
This lesser miracle, taking place against a background of
entropy, is unanticipated: it strikes us with the force of a real
miracle, as if to suggest that through this persona's
association with his cave, in spite of the cycle of plenitude and
loss, something has survived. Briefly, the enclosed space of
the poem gives way to horizontal motion, the spirit's journey,
aimless perhaps, across roads which lead away from the
seaside setting, toward another more distant horizon.
Rhythmically, this passage conveys a closured effect, a sense
of finality which makes lines 86-103 seem a coda rather than an
ending. Since this passage works as the climax of the poem,
we should be at some pains to decide whether this miracle is to

be taken positively, as an affirmative conclusion, or as a renewed statement of despair. Are we witnessing the resurrection of the magician figure, or a further disintegration of his role? We start with the *khiraq* ("rags") which rise from the magician's corpse, and watch the adventures of that entity as it shuttles back and forth on an axis between being and nonbeing. The word *khirqa* itself is ambiguous: as with the question we asked about the cave, does the image emphasize the tatters or the cloth in which the tatters are worn? The verb *tabakhkharat* ("melts away") suggests its dissolution; *takawwarat* ("takes a spherical shape") suggests its solidification, but what does it solidify into? A *shabah* ("spirit, ghost"), again an image of the intangible. The intangible assumes a volitional act of movement, *yamdi* ("*mada*, go forth, set out"), but the final verb encapsulates its motion in the passive: in the syntax of the Arabic text, the roads "unfurl" it, "shake it off" (*tanfudu*) from one place to another. We see the verb *tanfudu* as crucial, first because it reinforces the image of cloth (*khiraq*), which first put the success of the resurrection into question, second because the motion described in the word *nafada* is like the motion of a road (does a road move? yes and no), unwinding, extending from a fixed point, an image (unlike *yamdi*) which combines motion and stillness. It is the motion of unwinding cloth: one end remains fixed. A series of oppositions have been marvelously superimposed: being and non-being, motion and stillness, the contradictory success and failure of the poetic process. Inspiration has come and gone. Whatever remains is represented in a paradoxical resurrection which is compromised at every turn.

In the lines which act as a coda (ll. 86-103), the persona hears his mother's voice calling him to society, which exists behind the cave, in the direction away from his uncanny relationship with the bestowing "thou." The temptation of the mother's voice (ll. 89-92) is an alternative conclusion to the cycle, another example of horizontal motion, this time to "a field, a plow," but he refuses to leave his place of exile. (Is it also a temptation to conventional modes of art, since to field and plow he adds, incongruously, *maktaba*, "library," here translated "world of books"?) His kingdom is in the cave which faces the sea; his choice is between the madness of conformity (going back to his mother's existence) and submission to his current state, which, in its way another kind of madness, represents his only glimmer of hope, the only possibility of renewed vision. In this context, then, his tragic acceptance of:

> . . . A hungry cave, a wasted yawning mouth,
> A hollow hand that drags and draws the hollow line
> Only to wipe it out with slow tepidity

is a return to the beginning, to self-imposed exile, to the mundane situation of the poet sitting in front of an empty page. The metaphoric atmosphere is the same as that of the opening lines, but a specific metaphoric dimension has been foregrounded: that of the act of inscription. The transposition of modifier ("a wasted yawning mouth," "hungry cave") does more than express emptiness and desolation: by describing cave in terms of mouth and vice-versa it makes the cave an agent of poetry, the organ metonymically associated with verbal creation. We are back at the moment of desolation where we began, but with the difference that the metaphorical context has been sharpened. The surprise becomes a recognition. The hand devoid of substance is still afflicted with absence ("a hollow hand") but it is a hand which, though the act is equivocal and compromised, has created something like itself, "a hollow line." It is here that the theme of creative power is explicitly particularized as poetic creation; it surfaces momentarily, but in retrospect it is latent in the whole poem.

The cave is what everyone says it is: the solitude of the artist, the exile of the self from society, a shelter in times of spiritual emptiness, but it is now most prominently superimposed on hand, mouth and "line" (khatt), creator (as writer and orator) and created (the poem), and all are in a state of depletion. It is profoundly reflexive: a mimesis of its own begetting, its birth, even of the inevitable failure of poetry to embody the identity with which it was conceived. There is an inevitable paradox imbedded in the project of writing about inspiration.

The aspect of the poem which we mean to emphasize is hermeneutially prior to the social contexts. Before it is about the condition of the Arab world in the fifties it is about inspiration in a universal sense, a sense which involves it in a series of paradoxical issues. Presumably inspiration precedes

the poem as a creative act: to see it engulfed in the content of
the poem is to look into the gears of the poetic process in a
kind of poetic primal scene. A discontinuous process, only
partly volitional, is portrayed as part of the "plot" of the
poem. We do not see prosaic thoughts turn into poetic ones.
Even when Hawi depicts the absence of inspiration, the
diction and texture are no less poetic. This tradition of look-
ing inward to the origins of inspiration may be as old as the
depiction of the rainstorm in the *Mu'allaqa* of Imru' al-Qays.
In English romanticism it becomes a central theme. Word-
worth's "I wander'd lonely as a cloud," where the vision of
the daffodils is a window into the creation of the poem, is
perhaps the textbook example. Shelley's image of the fading
coal in his *Defense of Poetry*, the classical critical statement,
suggests that the moment of inspiration is always imperfectly
represented. The imperfect nature of the representation is
emphasized in the esthetic of French *symbolisme* and the
moment commemorated is consequently not the moment of
conception or inspiration but a later point in the process, the
moment of inscription where the pure idea is compromised
by its expression in words. The poetry of Mallarmé be-
queathes this idea to the twentieth century, where it is
latent in contemporary esthetics, from Yeats and Valéry to
Montale and Jabes. It does not seem fruitful to speak of in-
fluences; to see Hawi as a participant in a tradition is simply
to make him a poet of his time. What is new in Hawi's con-
ception of inspiration is the particular role he assigns to the
will: inspiration is an act of grace but this does not make the
poet's role passive. He waits for inspiration, but he chooses
to wait for it, despite the risk of madness such waiting entails.
Without inspiration there is no justification even for waiting.

Notes

[1]*After Babel* (New York, 1975): 277.

[2]Muta' Safadi, "*Bayadir al-Ju' 'an al-mu'anat wa al-mas'uliyya*,"
al-Adab 7 (July, 1965): 8-10, 60-66.

[3]Hani al-Rahib, "Hiwar hawla *Bayadir al-Ju'*," *al-Adab* 8 (August,
1965): 65-68.

[4]*A Critical Introduction to Modern Arabic Poetry* (London, 1975):
249.

[5]*Muqaddima li-al-shi'r al-'Arabi* (Beirut, 1971): 13.

[6]A. J. Arberry, *An Introduction to the History of Sufism* (London, 1942): xvii.

The Genie of the Beach

جنّية الشاطئ

في خيم الغجر المشرعة للريح ، والمبحرة مع الريح ، تعرى الذات عن حيوية الفطرة والبراءة الاولى . والحيوية اعياد مرح تنبع من الذات الفياضة وتنسكب فيها . والبراءة حال الانسان الاول في ظل شجرة الحياة قبل ان تغريه حلاوة المعرفة ومرارتها في شجرة الخير والشر فيطرده سيف النار من الجنة .

لذلك كانت ذات الغجرية خير رمز للحيوية المندفعة، ولشجرة الحياة : « تفاحة الوعر الخصيب » ، ولقدرة الانسان في حال البراءة على الاندماج بعناصر الحيوية في الطبيعة :« وعول الجبل رخيول البحر » .

ويسبغ الشاعر على الغجرية اوصافاً رحبة معممة ترمز الى الارض في تجدد حيويتها وفي بكارتها الدائمة .

وفي المدينة يعصى على الغجرية فهم الشريعة وشجرة المعرفة:

« أتعبّ غير رطوبة الحمى وتعقدها ثمر ؟ » وتلتقي الكاهن الموسوي حارس تلك الشجرة فيمتحنها بالنار وبشريعة لا تسري عليها .

والكاهن رمز الذات والحضارة معاً في حال الاحتقان الذي يحوّل الحيوية الى كبريت ونار مجرمة . لقد رمى الغجرية بالاثم والشر والمنفى الى حيث اصيبت بالجنون ، فظنت ان حكمه صدق وعدل وانها بالفعل جنية وروح شريرة . وكان في جنونها براءة موجعة .

(Hawi's introduction to "Jinniyyat al-shati' ")

In gypsy tents, open to the winds, travelling with the winds, the self (al-dhat) unveils the vitality of instinct (fitra) and original innocence. Vitality is the feasts of joy which issue from overflowing self and pour into it. Innocence is the state of the first man in the shade of the Tree of Life, before the sweetness and bitterness of knowledge in the Tree of Good and Evil tempted him. And so the sword of fire evicts him from Paradise.

For this reason the self of the gypsy is the best symbol for both this unbridled vitality and for the Tree of Life, "the apple of the fertile wild," as well as for the ability of man in the state of innocence to coalesce with the elements of vitality in nature: "mountain stags and seahorses."

The poet clothes the gypsy in wide, general descriptions that symbolize earth in its renewed vitality and in its eternal virginity.

In the city the gypsy is incapable of understanding either the code (al-shari'a) or the Tree of Knowledge. "What could it [her body] feed on but its fever's sweat/To make it shoot and bud and carry fruit?" She meets the Mosaic priest, the guardian of that tree, who tries her with fire and with codes that do not apply to her. The priest is the symbol of civilization and the self together, in a state of congestion (ihtiqan) that transforms vitality to brimstone (kibrit) and transgressing fire. He has cast upon the gypsy sin, evil and exile, so that she is afflicted with madness. She thought that his judgment was honest and fair, and that she herself was indeed a genie and an evil spirit. There was in her madness a painful innocence.

١ ــ خيم الغجر

هل كنتُ غير صبية سمراء
في خيم ٱلغجرْ ،
خيم بلا أرضٍ وأوتادٍ وأمتعةٍ تعيقْ ،
أُريحُ تحملها فتبحرُ
خلف أعياد ٱلفصولِ
تحطُّ من عيد لعيد في ٱلطريقْ
وٱلريحُ تمسح ما تخلّفهُ
ٱلعشية من أثَرْ
للهرجِ وٱلنيرانِ في خيم ٱلغجرْ

The Genie of the Beach

I. Gypsy Tents

That's All I've ever been—a dark-skinned girl
In gypsy tents that have no land, no pegs,
No chattels that impede, that carried by the wind
Sail on beyond the season's feasting days,
And land on wayward roads from feast to feast.   5
The wind wipes out the traces that are left
From flames and revels round the gypsy tents.

٢ ــ وعول الجبل وخيول البحر

هل كان في جسدي

سوى طبع ٱلرمال ٱلغضة

ٱلعطشى ، رمالْ

تشتفُّ عنف ٱلموج يمخرها

ويجتاح ٱلشواطىء وٱلمضيقْ

ماذا أيتبعني ٱلصدى عبر ٱلجبال ؟

وهناك عند شواطىء

ٱلثلج ٱلعريقْ

كأَنت ظلالُ ٱلحَورِ تحرقني

تشفُّ ضلوعه ٱلخضراء

عن جمرٍ تخمَّر في ٱلقرارْ

II. Mountain Stags and Horses of the Sea

And has there been incarnate in my flesh
Except the nature of the mellow sand,
The thirsty sand yearning with lusty want   10
For the outrageous fury of the waves,
Which furrow and assault the beaches and the straits?
Will echoes haunt me from the mountain range?
There on the coasts of the primeval snow
The shades of poplar burned my flesh;   15
Their verdant branches left unveiled
Fermented embers in my depths.

وأرى رؤى محرورةً طولَ ٱلنهارْ :

أشياءَ في برك ٱلدمِ

ٱلفوّار يحجبها بخارْ

ينزاح عن وعل يحرُّ عروقَ

عينَيهِ أحمرارْ

ويلحُّ في دفع ٱلوعولْ

ماذا أتعبرني ٱلوعولْ ؟

جسدي يئنُّ ، يضيقُ ، يلهثُ ، يستحيلْ

عَلَفاً ، تلالاً غضةً ، غوراً ، حقولْ ،

ألنعنعُ ٱلبريُّ يمرجُ في مطاوي

ٱلسفحِ

وٱلريحانُ أدغالاً بأوديتي يهيجْ

تلهو وتمرحُ فيه قطعان ٱلوعولْ

And feverish visions I beheld all day;
Things in the ponds of boiling blood,
Dim shapes in rising steam are veiled,   20
A raging stag looms into sight,
Rubbing its eyes blood red, routing the herd.
Will I be trampled by the raging stags?
My body moans, it cringes, pants, becomes
Mere fodder, meadows, verdant fields.   25
The wild mint wallows in the crannied mountain foot,
And in my valleys groves of pansies throng,
Both frenzied stags in wild abandonment

وتروح تمخره ، خيولُ البحرِ تزحمها خيولْ

تُرغي وتكتسح الخليجْ

ويظلُّ للجسد الطريِّ صفاء مرآةٍ

وعنقودٍ يجوهر في دَعَهْ

عبرتْ وما عبرتْ عليه الزوبعهْ

And horses of the sea surge through the pansied fields,
And galloping they race into the bay   30
Urged by their frothing mates, thrusting their way along.
Yet there remains within the tender flesh
The mirror's clearness and the glowing tan
Of tranquil rip'ning clusters of the vine,
Trodden by gales yet unaffected still.   35

٣ ـ في المدينة

هل كنتُ في ليل ٱلمدينةِ
غيرَ أعياد ٱلبيادرِ في ٱلحصادْ
تفاحةَ ٱلوعر ٱلخصيبِ ، وهبتُ
من جسدي ، دمي ،
خمراً وزادْ ،
وعجبتُ من جسد تلويهِ
وتعصرهُ سياجاتُ عشرْ
أيعبُّ غير رطوبةِ ٱلحمّى
ويعقدها ثمرْ ؟

III. In the City

And in the city's night what have I been
Except the harvest feast on threshing floors,
Except the apple of the fertile wild?
I offered of my flesh: blood, wine and bread.
And I behold with great perplexity   40
A body plied and squeezed by fetters ten.
What could it feed on but its fever's sweat
To make it shoot and bud and carry fruit?

4 ـ الكاهن الموسوي والدينونة

يرغي عليَّ ٱلاسودُ ٱلداجي

ٱلمقنَّع بٱلرماذ

وأرى خلال ٱلرغوةِ ٱلصفراءِ

كبريتاً تجمَّر في مغارَةْ

ويفوح محمرُّ ٱلحديدِ

ودخنةُ ٱللحم ٱلطريّ من أَنعبارَةْ :

« جسدُ ٱللعينةِ لن يطهِّره ٱلعماذ »

(وزَّعتُ من جسدي ، دمي)

(خمراً وزاذ)

IV. Moses' Priest and Doomsday

Shrouded in ash and robed in black,
He overwhelms me in his fuming froth;   45
And I see through the yellow froth a cave
Blazing in sulfur flames and blobbing red
In iron lava, surging heavily.
And emanating from the words he speaks
I see the smoke of burning pliant flesh: 50
"The body of the damned shall not be cleansed
Or purified in the baptismal font."
(I offered of my flesh: blood, wine and bread.)

أيشقُّ عن كبدي لينهشهَ ٱلغرابْ
كادت تمزّقني ٱلكلابْ ،
لليوم أرجف ، أُغمض العينينِ ..
أصرخ .. لا أُطيقْ
وتصيحُ في نهديَّ آثارُ ٱلحروقْ
وعلى ٱلطريقْ
جسدٌ يموت ويستفيقْ

Would he split up my heart, leave it a prey
To crows? The dogs had almost torn my flesh.   55
And still I shake with fear; I close my eyes,
I wail, I can endure no more . . .
And on my breasts, the scars of burns lament
And on the road, a body dies and wakes.

دمغتْ جبيني لعنةٌ حمراءُ

كانتْ من سنينَ ، وما تزالْ

يحكونَ : « لي جسد عجيبْ

ترتدُّ عنه ٱلنارُ ، ترتدُّ

ٱلخناجرُ وٱلنبالْ

يحكونَ :

أطبخُ في ٱلكهوفِ لحومَ أطفالِ

ولي عين أصيدُ بها ٱلرجالْ ،

وأموت حين أحسُّ رعب العابرينْ

وصدى لعينْ :

« بٱسم ٱلصليب لعلَّ يطردها ٱلصليبْ ،

V. The Brand of the Genie and Sin

Upon my brow damnation leaves its brand,   60
Its scarlet blaze unfaded through the years.
They say, "Her mystic body scorns the might
Of scorching fire and of rending steel."
They say, "She cooks in caves the flesh of babes,
And men fall prey to her alluring eyes."   65
A deadly dread engulfs me when I sense
The fright of people passing in the streets,
Or when their cursed voices say,
"The name of Jesus' cross might drive her off "

(تفاحةٌ غجريةٌ)

(وصيةُ ٱلوعر ٱلخصيبْ)

ما زلتُ أجهلُ ما ٱلذنوبُ وكيفَ
تغتَسلُ ٱلذنوبْ

وأخاف من « بٱسم الصليبْ »

أنسلُّ للكهفِ ٱلمعلَّقِ
فوق أمواج ٱلمضيقْ :

رملٌ ، نفاياتٌ ، كلابٌ ،

مرفأٌ خَرِبٌ عتيقْ .

(And I an apple, virgin of the fertile wild).   70
I do not comprehend the brand of sin
Or how the scarlet curse is purged and cleansed.
I dread that phrase "The name of Jesus' holy cross."
I steal my way into the cave
That overhangs the breakers of the straits: 75
Debris and dogs and sand, a wasted bay.

٦ - عجوز مجنونة

كانت بروقُ ٱلليل تلعبُ

في زوايا ٱلكهفِ تفرشه شَرَرْ

ـى وبردْ ، عتمةْ ، لَهَبْ ، خَدَرْ

أحببتُ حين صحوت تلكَ

ٱلدمغةَ ٱلحمراءَ تلمع في ٱلجبينْ ،

طربي لرعب ٱلعابرينْ ،

في ٱلليلِ أطبخُ لحم أطفالٍ ، يقينْ ،

في ٱلليلِ حين يفتَّح ٱلمرجانُ

في ضوء ٱلقمرْ

ينحلُّ لونُ جدائلي ٱلبيضا

ووجهي تمَّحي عنه ٱلحُفَرْ ،

VI. A Mad Old Woman

The lightning flashes of the night capered
And decked in flames the corners of the cave:
Fever and chills, darkness and flame and haze.
And when I stirred from the oppressive spell   80
I was enamored of the glist'ning scar
Branded upon my brow in scarlet hue,
And blazing out of my excessive joy
At seeing people gripped in fear.
Indeed, I cook the flesh of babes at night,   85
And in the moonlight, when the rubies bloom,
My white locks change their color, and the grooves
In my sad face are rubbed and levelled smooth.

عيدُ ٱلتجلّي حين أخلعُ

شجْرةَ ٱلخِرَقِ ٱلعتيقةِ

صَدَقةَ ٱلجسدِ ٱلعتيقْ

وأروح أهزج في ٱلطريقْ :

تفاحةُ ٱلوعرِ ٱلخصيبِ ، صبيّةٌ

سمراءُ من خيم ٱلغَجَرْ

قلبُ ٱلصباح يشعُّ من نهديَّ ،

عنقودُ ٱلدرَرْ ،

ومع ٱلسحَرْ

ألهو ، يطيبُ لي ٱلتنكرُ ،

أتّقي ٱللَّعَناتِ ، أسخرُ بٱلبشَرْ

هيهات يُعرفَ مَنْ أنا ، عبثاً ، مُحالْ ،

شمطاءُ تنبش في ٱلمزابلِ

عن قشور ٱلبرتقال .

Transfiguration day is soon at hand,
When I shake off the ancient tree of rags,   90
The hardened shell of old imprisoned flesh,
And then exultant on the road I shout:
I am the apple of the fertile wild,
A dark-skinned girl from wayward gypsy tents,
The morning finds its heart within my breast   95
And from its lustre borrows all its light.
Then with the dawn I revel in my masks,
Avoid the curses, mock the human race.
In vain they seek my true identity,
A beldame searching dumps for orange peels.   100

Three Interpretations of
"The Genie of the Beach"

We begin with a q tation from Jabra Ibrahim Jabra:

"And upon reading it [Hawi's "Jinniyyat al-shati' "] a query comes to mind: is it necessary that the gypsy be a symbol for anything other than herself? Isn't her sensuous image enough? . . . why this insistence on symbols, when they are not necessary? We should not think symbolically except when we have failed to realize the wide, flowing, complex meaning—to realize it in the symbol itself. Otherwise, we do well to hold fast to the sensuous image itself, to the direct image that is nothing but itself. The beauty of "The Genie of the Beach" will not be restored unless the poem is taken as nothing but itself. It divulges its own meaning, and any attempt by the poet to analyze it is uncalled for."[*]

The function of this passage is to separate Hawi's comment from the text of his poem. Why separate them? We are in the unusual situation of knowing in advance what the poem "means," that is — as the undergraduate phrase has it — what the poet "meant to say." Is this a reader's aid or a means

[*](Jabra Ibrahim Jabra, "Monologue, Montage and Allusion," *Al-Rihla al-thamina* "The Eighth Voyage," Beirut, 1967, pp. 62-63.)

of intimidating the critics?[1] Our analysis is aware of the
paradox of original intention (evidently embodied in his
introduction) and final product: what the final product
may mean involves a series of strategies that the language
of poetry imposes upon original intention. These strategies
will not be bound by any one interpretation, not excluding
that of the poet himself. (Thus far we are on Jabra's side.)

It is doubtful that gypsies are in fact beyond the repressive
morality Hawi attacks, or that a Rousseauian view of nature
and the natural man will help us unravel the shifts of scene and
identity which characterize the poem. It does seem clear that
city versus wild reflects a dichotomy between innocent and
fallen. The state of innocence exists only in exile, in gypsy
tents, i.e., outside the settled, civilized world. Despite the
erotic passages of part two, in part one the gypsy's innocence
is subject to renewal ("The wind wipes out the traces" — line
6). The figure of the gypsy in western literature is romantic and
positive; for the Arab reader an opposed set of associations
will arise: the gypsy as thief and kidnapper of children. (The
western view of the gypsy is rather more like the Arab view of
the Bedouin — whose communion with the desert makes him
a symbol of freedom and spontaneity.) As a symbol, therefore,
the gypsy betrays the Arab reader's expectations. The
speaker herself is aware of this irony. (We take the phrase,
"Indeed, I cook the flesh of babes at night" [line 85] to be ironic
and mocking rather than confessional.) The characterization
of her identity in the concluding lines as a series of masks (lines
97-98) is hard to reconcile with Hawi's statement in his
introduction to the poem that she comes to believe the priest's
judgment of her. Indeed, the gypsy of the poem seems a more
resilient figure than the gypsy of Hawi's synopsis. (Is this the
difference between original intention and the language of
poetry?)

The issue is the nature of the gypsy's fall from innocence. It
is the result not of sexual experience but of repression. Her
awareness of coherent identity through her transformations is
an important aspect of the poem's own coherence. The
synopsis, on the other hand, emphasizes the fragmentation of
self. There are clearly two stages: one in which she is the girl at
home in the natural world (tent, sands), another in which her
symbol is the old Gypsy beldame — whose home is (as in the

previous poem) a cave by the ocean. The erotic vision in part
two seems to describe oneness with nature, a scene of
wholeness and unfallen sexuality, what Hawi terms
"unbridled vitality" (*Al-hayawiyya al-mundafi'a*).

The panorama in part two is predicated upon a series of
polarities which are densely interwoven and complex; the
syntax meanwhile is so straightforward and simple that we are
tempted to read through it without reflection. The first term of
the polarities is the sand, which is at once stage-setting and a
metaphor of the gypsy's own body. Sand is itself an unstable
signifier: it is both a hostile environment (unstable surface,
desert scene) and a sensuous texture (often compared in form
to a woman's body), common to desert and seaside. The
gypsy characterizes herself (or her body — the point may be
that for her the two, body and self, are not distinct) by two
contradictory features of sand — its mellowness and ripeness
(*ghadd*) and its thirst (*'atash*). She invokes it as a generalized
substance; immediately it becomes a more or less specific
geographical scene. The camera pulls back: we visualize the
sand extending beyond the horizon to the sea. Thus the
representation of her being (*tab'*) suggests both wholeness
and longing, stillness and motion. (The juxtaposition of those
opposites is typical of Hawi.) Self and sea are terminal points
of desire, mediated by sand. A second opposition links self and
mountains. Here the mediating agent is sound ("Will echoes
haunt me from the mountain range?" line 13); the mountains,
like the sea, are referred to as a "coast," but a coast
characterized by cold and stillness, snow instead of ocean.
The relation gypsy/beach and gypsy/mountain is a strange
polarity which breaks down over the course of two visions
(lines 14-17 and 19-31). The first is a memory which merges
heat and cold: "**The shades of poplar burned my flesh;**/their
verdant branches left unveiled/fermented embers in my
depths (lines 15-17). (The image recalls the green embers of
"The Cave.") She becomes even more plainly the site of
polarities which break down in the second erotic vision, where
first she merges with the mountain landscape and then is
violated by the emblematic animals of both scenes, mountain
stags and horses of the sea. The following schemata portray
these relationships visually:

Lines 14-17

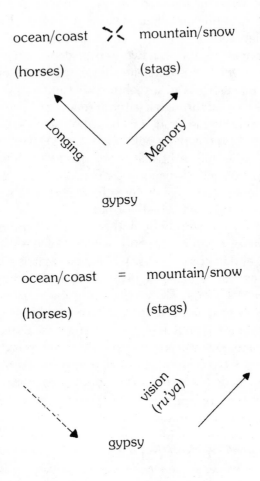

Lines 19-31

The first triangle is a set of static relationships. The second is the site of a narrative, in which the gypsy first sees and is then violated by the emblematic animals. The mediating agent is her transformation into the landscape — an episode of intense sensuality. Her awareness of the stags' potential violence (lines 21-23), the physical symptoms of desire (24) and her merging with the soil (with the peculiar, erotically ambiguous detail of the wildflowers) gradually establish a mood of passivity which anticipates the act of violation. The words "merging" and "identification" are blunt instruments to describe the numerous subtle shadings of relationship between elements of this episode. The leg of the second triangle which connects gypsy and mountain represents first her vision of the mountain scene, but of course at line 24 she becomes (or imagines herself) a part of that scene, thus opening herself to the violation which ensues, which brings our attention to the leg of the triangle connecting mountain and coast. We have marked that leg with an "equals" sign to indicate the merging of mountain stags with horses of the sea, along with the merging of mountain and ocean scenes. We should add that the "equals" sign should not be understood to obliterate the respective identities of shore and mountain. In a sense the gypsy has moved, via vision, through trans- formation, then by violation, along two legs of the triangle, traversing (through the imagined sexual act) in lines 19 to 31 the same course she designated in lines 10-12, in the act of longing attributed to the sand. Perhaps, rather than traversing the legs of the triangle, she contains them, since it is clear from lines 32-35 that the Keatsian serenity of the original version ("Of tranquil rip'ning clusters of the vine," line 34) remains intact through the act of violation — in a narrative which combines motion and stillness (again) in the manner of "The Cave." Ultimately, therefore, the journey continues across the third leg of the triangle back to self — all lines of demarcation between violence and serenity having been transcended. The sensual gypsy which Jabra would have us enjoy is undeniably present, but it falsifies the situation to call her simply a sensuous image. Does the sensuality originate in the presumed physicality of the image or in the sensual rhythm with which the erotic is conveyed, the delicate intersection of being and non-being which makes it at once present and elusive, ornamented and unclothed, a scene and a com- mentary on its own fictionality?

In the first two sections the gypsy is portrayed as a natural force in unison with the plant and animal forces of nature. The relationship is one of wholeness — a pagan relationship to nature, drawing upon the complex of forest and wild imagery we associate in English literature with Keats (in Arabic particularly with Gibran and Hawi). The perspective which follows draws on a Miltonic (perhaps Blakean?) sensibility in which innocence is not intuited but rather defined by its opposites in a fallen world. It is impossible to miss that the gypsy is a sacrificial figure (she is herself "the harvest feast on threshing floors" who offers her own body, lines 37, 39). Without pushing the identification to extremes, we may suggest that the loss of innocence applies to any number of sacrificial heroes catalogued in Frazer's *Golden Bough*, among whom Jesus is the most relevant. It is as if the harvest feasts (*a'yad al-bayadir fi al-hasad*) were the point where there is a virtual meeting between city life and nature, the intersection of the gypsy's life and that of the settled community. As the word *bayadir*, "threshing floors," occurs in the title of the *diwan*, it assumes an added importance; the threshing floors in the title yield hunger (*bayadir al-ju'*), and the gypsy's estrangement in the city implies the city's own inability to accept its own relation to natural forces. Two Biblical narratives, one from the Old Testament and one from the New, seem to have been superimposed on one another: the fall from innocence in the Eden story and the sacrifice of Jesus. It is as if the fall occurred to an Adam and Eve who remain guiltless.

Hawi's synopsis draws our attention to the Biblical story of the fall, but at the expense of not acknowledging what the poem leaves out. Unstated is the cause, the psychological mechanics of the fall in the Bible story. This is not a Miltonic account: the fall takes place offstage, somewhere between lines 39 and 40. It is not the result of a greed for knowledge; it simply happens, like the cycle of transformations in Blake's "Mental Traveler." In fact, the gypsy's fall seems to be unavoidable; its product is not knowledge, for she remains ignorant of sin and its purification (lines 71-72). (A von Grunebaum or some other Western apologist might see this as the confrontation of a shame culture and a guilt culture.) The city becomes not just a place, but the self-awareness which is the fallen state of mind. The gypsy's fall we see as synonymous with her entry into the city, or into a repressive awareness of self. Her perplexity over the ten fetters (Arabic *siyajatun 'ashar*, "ten fences," line 41) is presented with characteristic narrative indirection. We do not see them being clamped on; she discovers herself in captivity. Nor are we told explicitly that it is her body she sees confined: the result is to universalize the confinement, a juxtaposition of a concrete universal which recalls Blake's "mind-forg'd manacles" in the poem "London" or the golden net which traps the soul in the poem of that name. The number ten, which may seem arbitrary in part three, becomes clearer in the explicit religious context of part four. In a sense there is a distinction between the Old Testament's insistence on the commandments (the ten fetters) and the New Testament's commitment to the living word. In St. Paul's words, "For without the law, sin was dead," and, "for I was alive without the law once: but when the commandment came, sin revived and I died." (Romans 7. 7-9).

Political contexts, like theological ones, loom on every side of the reader's experience in "The Gypsy of the Beach." The imagery of innocent versus fallen worlds lends itself to political frameworks, and a common reading of Hawi sees the figures of the poet in "The Cave" or the gypsy here as representatives of a new, more natural social order. The polarities between the speaker's innocent self and her city self, between apple of the fertile wild and old woman, between youth and age, between innocence and experience, are all potentially conflicts with a hard didactic edge. To the extent that the gypsy's desert existence represents values opposed to the fallen world of the city, values which not so much oppose them as negate them and deny their validity, we can see her as an agent of aggression against authority, and she is to that extent an image of rebellion. The reader does not feel here, as in "Lazarus," the third poem of *Bayadir al-Ju'*, that specific references to the Arab cultural and political scene are clamoring to be heard above more textual and reflexive contexts. This can be seen more clearly if we focus on the priest who is the gypsy's antagonist, our specific villain in the piece. The function of the figure of the priest is a concretion of the fall we have already glimpsed in part three. He is the source of a vision through smoke to contrast the erotic vision (first seen through steam) in part two. The priest, by offering us a specific villainous figure, represents a temptation for the critic to fall into an overly specific mode of interpretation. (In this respect he is the agent of fallen vision for the critic as well

as the gypsy, and perhaps, we shall suggest, for Hawi too.)
Between the specificity of Biblical allusion in Hawi's synopsis
and the autonomous coherence of the poem there is a
distance in which the reader must locate him or herself.
Without the synopsis we could recognize the more or less
Gothic myth of the innocent female victimized by a figure of
authority (the priest), representative of a sinister environment
(the city), the story of the innocent in exile who is perceived as
an aggressor. Specific Biblical elements in the poem are
unmistakably less pervasive than in the synopsis. Do we need
the Tree of Life to explain the term "apple of the fertile wild?"
Do we need the Tree of Knowledge to explain the role of
the Mosaic priest? We have the reference to the cross
of Jesus (line 69), which is an unusual moment in the poem (we
will suggest others below) when the gypsy's point of view
pauses and allows us to hear a concrete outside voice, but that
moment may strike us more as a moment of realism than a
contribution to the allegorical structure, a moment of
mirroring when she hears herself described from outside. In a
sense the narrative motion of the poem is from a generalized
presentation to the specific situation of the old woman in the
cave, from a visionary to a realistic mode. A realistic world
closes in around us. The poem's difficulty is the confusion
between the woman's transformation and the transformation
in our perception of her. We might describe her fall as simply
her transformation into a specific character — from idealized
gypsy to naturalistic beldame (from gypsy to genie), from
young woman to old, from desert-dweller to troglodite, the
shore which was the site of desire in part two becoming,
ironically, the site of her exile in part five.

   As interpreters we wish to preserve the continuum between
the concrete situation which concludes the poem and the
series of tableaux, more fluid and shifting, which precede it.
There is a temptation to anchor the poem on a particular level.
For instance, the mad old woman of part six could logically be
made the speaker of the entire poem, and the leitmotif, "that's
all I've ever been" (in Arabic a rhetorical question, hal kuntu
ghayra etc.) is a way of signaling a break in her perception of
temporal reality. This may lead an interpreter to view the
poem as an insane monologue in which the brute, ugly reality

which materializes at the end of the poem cancels out the visions of innocence that led to it. Hawi's insistence on a synopsis which encapsulates the poem on a single level of theological allegory, preserving the independence of the visionary tableaux at the expense of a single intellectual signification, is another such temptation. Jabra's insistence on the physical image, likewise, confines the reader's total experience of the poem. Our reading of part two was intended to demonstrate that the sensual level itself unfolds only through an intellectual process (of the sort that can be visualized drily, geometrically, structurally, as in the triangles above). Had we wished to examine the speaking persona more closely still we could have found multiple voices at work as early as part one: who speaks lines 2 to 7 of the poem? Dramatically it should be the gypsy, but the temporal and spatial widening of perspective, which shows us the tents as from a distance and summarizes the gypsy's migrations in general terms, suggests an outsider's voice, the voice of a third person narrator.

We have suggested in our discussion of the priest that the villain of the piece is concrete, anchored, particular vision, the vision represented by city and civilizational forces. The poet, by mediating between the universal and the concrete image plays dangerously with the temptations of fallen, concretized, fettered vision. The heroism of "The Genie of the Beach" is Hawi's attempt to maintain that mobility, to move freely between tableaux of fluid vision and the ultimate concrete manifestation of his ending. The gypsy's polyvalent being is an epilogue of the poem's dilemma. The desert is the site of marks which disappear ("The wind wipes out the traces," line 6). Its substance, sand, in the second part, is the mediator of self and shore. The city is the site of rules, commandments, traces which are preserved, such as the scarlet brand upon her body (breast or brow) associating the city with judgment. All acts of reading are unfortunately (perhaps inevitably?) attempts to confine meaning in permanent traces, to commit interpretative violence simply because the act of making sense out of complexity necessarily simplifies and reduces the experience. Hawi's epigraph is one such act; Jabra's objection is another. Our reading may be a third in ways we do not perceive.

Something about the text of "Genie of the Beach" invites
interpretive violence as the gypsy invites her violation in part
two. What is this quality which makes such extratextual
appendages as the synopsis and the titles to the individual
parts seem appropriate? The six minor titles offer us an
opportunity to examine the act of interpretive violence in the
most simple and germinal form. "Gypsy Tents," the first title,
names a setting we could have learned from the text. The
second, "Mountain Stags and Horses of the Sea," functions
more interestingly to isolate the natural agents of violation and
eroticism which, since they are detachable and visual images,
suggest the tangible and physical quality of the passage more
plainly than, say, "The Clear Mirror" or "Two Visions" might
have done. "In the City," the title of part three, designates a
setting, like "Gypsy Tents," but in its seeming blandness
perhaps universalizes, perhaps suggests the apocalyptic
overtones of the unreal city in Eliot's "Waste Land." The titles
of parts four and five, "Moses' Priest and Doomsday" and
"The Brand of the Genie and Sin" bring us closer to the world
of Hawi's synopsis, giving us information not in the text itself.
Without the one we would not know who the man robed in
black is in part four; the other is the only occurrence of the
word "genie," other than in the title of the poem. Both are in
the form of a concrete and an abstract noun from the
vocabulary of theology. In the sequence of titles we observe a
motion from more or less neutral markers ("Gypsy Tents,"
"Mountain Stags and Horses of the Sea") to interpretive
markers which charge their respective passages with
signification and at the same time drain them of discrete
coherence. The reference to the Mosaic priest in the fourth
title is like a floodgate through which a flow of scriptural
allusions inundate part four, but in the process the generalized
image (the man robed in black) is submerged. In the title of
part three meaning flows the other way, from passage to title,
this being perhaps more like the titles to "The Waste Land" in
which common phrases ("A Game of Chess") are elucidated
and take on added meaning from their context. The potential
hostility between title and passage becomes momentarily
explicit (and concrete) in the title to part six, "A Mad Old
Woman." If the woman is mad, the poem is an insane
monologue. If the title is ironic (like the phrase "Indeed I cook

the flesh of babes at night"), it puts into question the seeming neutrality of the voice who speaks the titles, as if to say "this is what they say about her, but we know better." In general, the habit of attaching overly informative titles to otherwise unfettered texts is a Western, European habit. The history of Arabic poetry leaves us texts whose titles are the product of random tradition: fragments of the first line or formal features of the verse line — signifiers which approach the arbitrary relation of word to signification with which Saussure characterizes language.

We do not wish to speak against the synopsis. (There is in English literary history alone a long history of synopses which have not deterred intelligent interpretation, from Spenser's letter to Raleigh to the prefatory summaries in *Paradise Lost*, from the headnotes Coleridge prepared for "The Ancient Mariner" to the notes, now considered ironic, which Eliot attached to "The Waste Land.") What sets Hawi's synopsis apart is the evident act of will which it represents, as if it were an alternative act of creation which almost supplants the poem. If we consider the titles which spring up in the ellipses and lacunae of the poem as germinal acts of interpretation, Hawi's synopsis is a further interpretive growth in which we see the poet attempting to regain control over an entity, the poem, which has cut loose from its original intention and will not go back. The beauty of the synopsis is that it is a concretion of certain tensions which are often latent in the poem's final form, but which poets rarely allow us to witness.

---

[1]Jabra of course was not intimidated, but he is the exception. See, for example, Muta' Safadi, *Bayadir al-Ju' 'an al-mu'anat wa al-mas'uliyya,"* *Al-Adab* (1965). 8-10; 'Ali Sa'd, "Naqd qasidat' Jinniyyat al-Shati' ," *Al-Adab* 8 (1961): 14; and Rita 'Awad, *Usturat al-mawt wa al-inbi'ath fi al-shi'r al-'Arabi al-hadith* (Beirut, 1978): 120.

Lazarus 1962

لعازر عام ١٩٦٢

« وذهبت مريم ، اخت لعازر، الى حيث كان الناصري
وقالت له لو كنت هنا لما مات أخي ،   فقال لها ان
اخاك سوف يقوم »

انجيل يوحنا

Lazarus 1962

And Mary, the sister of Lazarus, went unto the Nazarene and said to him: "Had you been here, my brother would not have died." And he told her: "Your brother will rise." (The Gospel of John)*

<hr />

*Not actually a quotation, but a conflation of John 11.20-23 and 11.32.

كنتَ صدى انهيار في مستهل النضال ، فغدوت ضجيج انهيارات حين تطاولت مراحله .

ثم راحت ملامحك تكوّن ذاتها في ذاتي ، وتعتصر من كل مناضل ينهار أخص صفاته وأعمها . كذلك راح الضجيج يستقر على صورة صافية الايقاع تشف عن اعماقه المتكرة .

ويوم تمّ تكوينك ، يوم طلعت من بخار الرحم ودخان المصهر ، كنت لعيني وجعاً ورعباً . حاولتُ ان اهدمك وابنيك . وكانت مرارات عانيتها طويلاً قبل ان انتهي عن رغبتي في ان تكون ابهى طلعة واصلب ايماناً واجلّ مصيراً . لئن كنتَ وجه المناضل الذي انهار في الامس ، فانت الوجه الغالب على واقع جيل ، بل واقع اجيال يُبتلى فيها القويّ الخيّر بالمحال فيتحوّل الى نقيضه ، ويتقمص « الخِضر » طبيعة « التنين » الجلاد والفاسق ، وتكون

المذلة مصدر تعاظمه :

« مارداً عاينتهُ يطلع من جيبِ السفيرْ » .

Hawi's Introduction to "Lazarus 1962"

You were the echo of breakdown at the outset of struggle, and you became the clamor of many breakdowns when the stages of struggle stretched.

Then your features started forming themselves within my own being, extracting from every defeated hero the most particular to the most general of his features. Then the clamor started to settle into an image of pure rhythm that unveiled its murky depths.

And on the day you finally took shape, on the day you emerged from steam of the womb and smoke of the foundry you became pain and horror to my eyes. I tried to destroy you and to rebuild you and as a result I suffered a prolonged bitterness before abandoning my desire that you be more beautiful, more steadfast and more glorious in destiny. And what then? If you are the face of the hero who broke down yesterday, then you are also the face that is seen everywhere, the reality of a whole generation, rather, generations, in which the powerful and the generous are smitten with vanity and are changed into their opposites: Saint George takes on the nature of the dragon-executioner and the depraved. His vices become the source of his glory:

> . . . a lurking giant coming forth
> out of the pouch of the Ambasador.

وهكذا ، وفيما يشبه الحدس ، اتحد الحاضر بكل زمان ، والواقع بالاسطورة ، فاكتسبت اسماً وكان الاسم جوهر كيانك : لعازر ، الحياة والموت في الحياة ، تموت القيم في المناضل وتسلم الحيوية فيكون الطاغية .

وما شأني إن تكن عناية الناصري ابت عليك ان تموت وانت بطل تراجيدي يتوهج بجلال التضحية ونشوتها بالجراح :

« مبحرٌ ، سكرانُ ، ملتفّ بزهر الارجوان »

وكيف تبعثك العناية وأنت « ميتٌ حجّرته شهوة الموت » وفي طبيعة الانبعاث ان يكون تفجراً من اعماق الذات ؟

وهذه امرأتك تلتقيك عائداً من الحفرة فيتولاها الرعب :

« ولماذا عادّ من حفرته ميتاً كئيبٌ »
« غيرُ عِرْقٍ ينزف الكبريتَ مسودّ اللهيبْ »

هي رمز الحياة ، عدت لتثأر منها لماض خيّر مبدّد ، وتجعلها على صورتك وتشدها الى مصيرك . ظلت تتهاوى الى ان بلغت

قرار جحيمك وحفرتك . نزفت في دمها الكبريت ، فارتدت عليك بالناب والمخلب .

And so, in something that resembles intuition, the present fused with the past and future, reality with legend. And you earned a new name, and the name was the essence of your being: Lazarus. Life and death-in-life. When ideals are destroyed within the hero and vitality is spared, the outcome is a tyrant.

I could only be helpless since the Nazarene's act of grace refused to allow you to die while you were a tragic hero enflamed with the glory of self-sacrifice and the ecstasy it takes in wounds:

> A drunken sailor robed in Tyrian red.

And how could the Nazarene's loving care resurrect you, you the corpse stiffened in the lust for death, since the nature of resurrection is that it be an explosion from the deepest recesses of the soul?

And here is your wife, meeting you on your way back from the grave. She is smitten with terror:

> Why did he leave his pit, a gloomy corpse
> dead but for one black sulphurous vein?

She is life itself. You came back to avenge yourself on her for a beneficent, dissipated past and to form her in your own image, to tie her to your fate. She kept on falling until she reached the depths of your hell and your pit. You breathed sulphur into her blood, and so she turned back at you with fang and claw.

كانت تنزع الى كمال وجودي يشبع النفس والجسد فخذلتها انت زوجها الحاقد الميت ، واسعفك الناصري بكماله الملائكي المترفع عن التجربة الحسية . لقد امتنعتْ عن الصلاة لاله لم يعرف الجوع ولا الافاعي المتولدة من شهوة متدافعة محتقنة :

« .. ما تُجدي الصلاةْ »

« لاله قمريّ ، ولِطيف قَمَريّ »

« يتخفّى في الغيوم الزرق في الضوء الطريْ »

« حيث لا يُرعدُ جوعٌ مارجٌ بالزفراتْ »

وبديهي ان يتعطل تطور الحياة متى انشقت الى مثالية غيبية ومادية متسفّلة ، متى تغوّرت الحيوية ، وخلع الوهم ظله المخدر على فجائع الواقع .

* * *

وبعد فانت لا تختصّ بجماعة دون جماعة
كنتُ شاهداً ورأيتك في صفوفهم جميعاً .

She yearned for a perfect life that would satisfy the hunger of body and soul, but you failed her, you her dead, resentful husband, and the Nazarene supplied your resentment with His angelic perfection which is disdainful of physical experience. She refused to pray for a God who had never experienced hunger or the serpents that grow out of a rushing yet bridled lust:

> How would my supplications and my tears
> affect a lunar god, a lunar ghost
> hiding in mellow light behind blue clouds
> where peals of hunger are inaudible?

It is self-evident that the progress of life is obstructed when life splits into a spiritual otherworldliness and a decadent materialism, when vitality seeps out and when illusion casts its opiate, numbing shadow upon life's catastrophes.

Therefore, you do not belong to one group rather than another. I was a witness. I saw you in the ranks of all of them.

١ - حفرة بلا قاع

عمّقِ ٱلحفرة يا حفّارُ ،

عمّقْها لِقاع لا قرارْ

يرتمي خلف مدار ٱلشمسِ

ليلاً من رمادٍ

وبقايا نجمة مدفونة خلف ٱلمدارْ

Lazarus

I. Bottomless Pit

Deepen the pit, gravedigger,
deepen it to bottomless depths
beyond the sun's orbit:
night of ashes, remnants of a star
buried in the wheeling abyss.   5

لا صدى يرشح من دوَّامة ٱلحمى

ومِن دولاب نارْ

آوِ لا تلقِ على جسمي

تراباً أحمراً حيًّا طري

رَحِماً يمخره ٱلشرش ويلتفُّ

على ٱلمَيْت بعنف بربري

ما ترى لو مدَّ صوبي

رأسه ٱلمحمومَ

لو غرَّق في لحمي نيوبَةْ

من وريدي راح يمتصُّ حليبَةْ

No echo from the vertigo of fever
nor from the flaming wheel.
O, do not cast live earth upon my corpse:
roots rip the sodden womb
and wrap the dead man savagely.   10
What if the roots should sprout their feverish heads?
What if they sink fangs into my flesh?
Suck milk from my veins?

لُفَّ جسمي ، لُفَّه ، حنِّطْه ، وَآطمِرْهُ

بكِلس مالحٍ ، صخرٍ من اَلكبريتِ ،

فحمٍ حجري

٢ ــ رحمة ملعونة

صلوات اَلحبِّ واَلفصح اَلمغنِّي

في دموع اَلناصري

أترى تبعث مِيتاً

ججَّرته شهوة اَلموتِ ،

ترى هل تستطيعْ

أن تزيحَ اَلصخر عنِّي

Wrap my corpse,
embalm it,   15
inter it,
in lime,
in sulphur stone,
petrified coal.

II. A Damnable Mercy

Prayers of love and chanting Easter Rhymes   20
In Jesus' tears, would they bring back to life
a dead man stiffened in the lust for death?
Could they from off my corpse remove the stone

والظلام اليابس المركومَ
في القبر المنيعْ ،
رحمة ملعونة أوجع من حمى الربيعْ
صلوات الحب يتلوها صديقي الناصري

·

كيف يحييني ليجلو
عَتمة غصَّت بها أختي الحزينةْ
دون أن يمسح عن جفنيَّ
حمّى الرعب والرؤيا اللعينةْ :

or shred the dense, dry darkness in my vaulted grave?
Those damned tears shed by my friend the Nazarene   25
are crueler than the fever of spring.

* * *

How could he resurrect me, to dispel
the dark that choked my sister in her grief,
without removing from my clouded eyes
the fever of fear, the damnable vision?   30

لم يزلْ ما كان من قبلُ وكان

لم يزل ما كانَ :

برقٌ فوق رأسي يتلوّى أفعوان

شارع تعبره الَغولُ

وقطعان الَكهوف المعتمَة

مارد هشَّم وجه الَشمسِ

عرَّى زهوها عن جمجمَة

عَتْمة تنزف من وهج الَثار ،

ألجماهير الَتي يعلكها دولابُ نارْ ،

وتموت الَنار في الَعتْمةِ ،

والَعَتْمة تنحلُّ لِنارْ

What has been is, what is has been unchanged:
lightning—snakes that writhe above my head;
a street where ghouls and sheep walk free,
their darkened caves abandoned;
a demon stripping layers from the sun,   35
who leaves its face stark naked, bares a skull;
a darkness bleeding from the glow of fruit;
thronging crowds chewed by the flaming wheels.
But flames into consuming darkness die
and darkness has reverted to flames.   40

٣ - الصخرة

أنبتِ اَلصخر ودعنا نحتمي

بأَلصخر من حمّى اَلدوار

سمّرِ اَللحظة عمراً سرمديًّا

جمّد اَلموج اَلذي يبصقنا

في جوف غول

إن تكن ربَّ اَلفصول .

واذا صوت يقول

III. The Rock

If you are the god of seasons, manifest
your strength, invest your rock with force to grow
and give us refuge from the dizzying gyre.
Perpetuate the fleeting moment
and freeze the waves that spew us forth   45
into a ghoul's belly.
And lo, a voice that said:

عبثاً تلقي ستاراً أُرجوانياً

على اَلرؤيا اَللعينَهْ

وبكت نفسي اَلحزينَهْ

كنتُ ميتاً بارداً يعبرُ

أسواق اَلمدينَهْ

أَلجماهير اَلتي يعلكها دولابُ نارْ

مَن أنا حتى أردَّ اَلنار عنها واَلدوارْ

عمَّقِ اَلحفرة يا حفَّارُ ،

عمَّقها لقاعٍ لا قرارْ .

"The damned vision shall not fade
even if masked with veils of "Tyrian red."*
I cried; I was a walking corpse   50
adrift in city streets.
The thronging crowds are chewed by flaming wheels.
Who am I to protect them from the rage
of fitful eddies and of gulping flames?
Deepen the pit, gravedigger,   55
deepen it to bottomless depths.

---

*"Tyrian red": *urjuwan*, the dye extracted from the murex by the
Phoenicians, used extensively by the Romans.

٤ – زوجة لعازر بعد اسابيع من بعثه

كان ظلاًّ أسوداً

يغفو على مرآة صدري

زورقاً مَيْتاً

على زوبعة من وهجٍ

نهديَّ وشَعري

كان في عينيهِ

ليلُ ٱلحفرة ٱلطينيُّ يدوي ويموجْ

عبر صحراءَ تغطّيها ٱلثلوجْ

IV. Lazarus' Wife a Few Weeks After His Resurrection

He was a shadow robed in black
reposing on the mirror of my breasts,
a dead skiff tempest-tossed amidst the rage
that issues from my glowing breasts and hair.   60
And in his eyes his hearse's ashen night
rumbled and rolled across a snow-clad waste.

عبثاً فتشت فيها

عن صدى صوتي وعن وجهي

وعينيَّ وعمري .

كان من حينٍ لحينٍ

يعبر الصحراءَ فولاذٌ محمّى ،

خنجرٌ يلهث مجنوناً وأعمى

نَمِرٌ يلسعه الجوع فيرغي ويهيجْ

يلتقيني علفاً في دربهِ

أُنثى غريبَهْ

يتشهّى وجعي ، يُشبع

من رعبي نيوبَهْ ،

In vain, I sought my echo there.
In vain, I sought my eyes, my face, my life.
From time to time, across the waste, there came   65
a blazing dagger, blind, panting, mad,
a slobbering tiger bit by hunger's teeth.
Enraged, he meets me in his way, fodder,
a woman unfamiliar—my pain his pleasure,
my fear the satisfaction of his fangs.   70

كَنتُ أَسترحم عينيهِ

وفي عينيَّ عارُ أَمرأةٍ

أَنَّتْ ، تعرَّتْ لغريبْ

ولماذا عاد من حفرتهِ

ميتاً كئيبْ

غيرُ عِرْقٍ

ينزف الكبريت مسودَّ اللهيبْ

I pled with him, I begged his distant eyes
to pity in my eyes a woman's shame,
who moaned, undressed before a stranger's eyes.
Why did he leave his pit, a gloomy corpse,
dead but for one black sulphurous vein?   75

٥ ـ زخرف

جارتي يا جارتي
لا تسأليني كيف عاذ
عاد لي من غربة ٱلموت ٱلحبيبْ
حجر ٱلدار يغنِّي
وتغنِّي عَتَبَات ٱلدار وٱلخمرُ
تغنِّي في ٱلِجرارْ
وستار الحزن يخضرُّ
ويخضرُّ ٱلجدارْ ،
عند باب ٱلدار ينمو ٱلغار ، تلتمُّ ٱلطيوبْ
عاد لي من غربة ٱلموت ٱلحبيبْ ،

V. Ornament

Do not ask, my dear dear friend,
how my love returned to me.
My love came back from his exile
in the land of death and waste.
In our house the happy stones   80
with the threshold sing in glee.
In our jars enchanted wine
joins the chorus joyfully.
Veils of sorrow shed their gloom,
reveling in the newest green   85
And the stones recall the days
of their verdant canopies:
by the door the laurel bloom
and perfumed breeze prevails.
My love came back from his exile   90
in the land of death and waste.

زندُهُ من بيلسانٍ حول خصري ،

زندُهُ يزرع نبض ٱلوردةِ

ٱلحمرا بعمري

بعد أن رمّد في ليل ٱلحداذْ ،

من يظنّ ٱلموت محواً

خلّهِ يحصي على ٱلبيدرِ

غلّاتِ ٱلحصاذْ

ويرى وجه حبيبي

وحبيبي كيف عاذْ

عاد لي من غربة ٱلموت ٱلحبيبْ

His arms like strings of pansies wrap my waist,
plant the throbbing of the rose
ember red in my sad life,
once ashes in my mourning nights.   95
He who holds that death is bane,
let him count on threshing floors
heaps of grain, the harvest yield;
let him see my lover's face,
how he came from his exile   100
in the land of death and waste.

(كنتُ أسترحم عينيهِ)

(وفي عينيَّ عار أمرأةٍ)

(أنتْ ، تعرَّت لغريبْ)

(ولماذا عاد من حفرتهِ)

(مَيتاً كئيبْ)

(غيرُ عِرْق ينزف الكبريتَ)

(مسودَّ اللهيب)

٦ ـ « الخضر ، المغلوب

ولماذا لم يعد يشتفُّ ما في
صدريَ الريّانِ من حبٍّ تصفّى وأختمَرْ ،

(I pled with him; I begged his distant eyes
to pity in my eyes a woman's shame,
who moaned, undressed before a stranger's eyes.
Why did he leave his pit a gloomy corpse,   105
dead but for one black sulphurous vein?)

VI. The Vanquished St. George*

Why does he long no more to quench his thirst
in the fermented love that settles clear
and undisturbed within my mellow breasts?

---

*In Arabic Hawi uses al-Khidr, a figure from Moslem tradition that
Arabic speaking Christians associate with St. George.

غيمةٍ تزهر في ضوءِ القمرِ

وسريرٍ مارجٍ بألموجِ

من خمرٍ وطيبٍ ،

جنةِ ٱلفُلْك على حمى ٱلدوارْ ،

طالما عاد الى صدري مرارْ

عاد مغلوباً جريحاً لن يطيبْ

ومدى كفَّيهِ أشلاءٍ من ٱلحقّ

مدى جبهته أشلاءٍ غارْ :

« حلوةٌ جُرَّت إلى ٱلتنين ، جُرَّتْ ، دُمِغَتْ

« للموت وأنهارت تعانيه أنتظارْ

The love that like a cloud blooms in moonlight   110
or like a bed rolling in scent and wine,
a paradise that rests in sweet repose
upon the fervent eddies of the Ark.
How often had he come back to my breasts.
vanquished, wounded and incurable,   115
wearing upon his forehead broken twigs
of laurels; in his hands remnants of truth:
"A fair maiden was chosen to appease
a dragon's wrath and suffer sacrifice,
but waiting for her death   120
she suffered death and died a thousand deaths.

، شكلُ كابوس ولا جسمْ
، وأشداقُ طواحين اَلشرَرْ
، مخلب نوَّب سيني
، غاص في صلب اَلحجَرْ ،
، مخلب في كبدي معولُ نارْ ،
، وعلى اَلشاطىءِ طفلٌ ناصريٌّ
، يغرس اَلبلسم في دنيا اَلقرارْ

A nightmare shape, if shape it might be called
that shape had none, its jaws satanic mills of flame:
my sword that pierces stone is blunted, lost
in formlessness—its grasping extremities
mattocks of flame which sear and rend my heart,
while on the beach a child, the Nazarene,
is digging shallow pits, planting his balsam
for the world to come.

125

٧ – عرس المغيب

» ما جنون ٱلدخنة ٱلحمراءِ

» في فجوةِ جرح لن يطيبْ

» لجريح يتلاشى في سرير ٱلموجِ

» من خمر وطيبْ

» تلتقيه ٱلشمس في عرس ٱلمغيبْ

» مبحرُ سكرانُ ملتفٌّ بزهو ٱلأرجوانِ

» عبثاً ترغي وترعي

» خلفه أشداقُ جانْ

» عبثاً ترشقه ٱلأرض بصمت مأتميٌّ

» ويكبُّ ٱلصخرَ في عينيهِ

» كابوسُ ٱلليالي

» نُتَفٌ من صحف ٱلأزياءِ

VII. Wedding at Day's End

"To what avail rages the sunset smoke   130
in a wound that will not heal,
to what avail to an afflicted man
collapsed on a bed rolling in scent and wine,
met by the sun at sunset wedding feasts,
a drunken sailor robed in Tyrian red.   135
In vain the genies spume and rage at him.
The earth rocks him in morbid silence, but in vain.
In vain nightmares set rocks upon his eyes.
Scraps of fashion magazines descend,

« تنهلُّ على وجهِ جريحِ لا يبالي ،

« لا يبالي

« بدمٍ ينزف مجنوناً سخيًّا ويروّي

« تربةً مصدوعةً يصدأُ فيها ويهانْ

« أو صدى الأجراسِ

« من جيل الى جيل يدوّي :

« كان سيفاً مورقاً ،

« جرحاً وينبوعاً وكانْ ،

« مبحرُ سكران ملتفٌّ بزهو الأرجوانْ

falling in shreds upon the face of one   140
wounded, listless and indifferent,
a man who hardly notices the blood
that gushes mad and swift to quench the thirst
of that rust-ridden land wherein he rusts
insulted and discredited.   145
A man who hears the echoes of the bells
which sing from age to age but pays no heed.
(He was a sword in leaf, a wound, a spring,
a drunken sailor robed in Tyrian red.)

« صدرُكِ ٱلرَّيَّان من جمرٍ ومن

« خمرٍ وطيبْ

« طالما طيَّب مغلوباً جريحاً لن يطيبْ

•

(كنتُ أسترحم عينيهِ)

(وفي عينيَّ عارُ أمرأةٍ)

(أنْتَ ، تعرَّتْ لغريبْ)

(ولماذا عاد من حفرتهِ)

(ميتاً كئيبْ)

(غيرُ عِرقٍ ينزف ٱلكبريتَ)

(مسودَّ اللهيبْ)

Your mellow breasts of amber, wine and scent   150
have often cured the wounds of injured men
who have been doomed and deemed incurable."

(I pled with him; I begged his distant eyes
to pity in my eyes a woman's shame,
who moaned, undressed before a stranger's eyes.   155
Why did he leave his pit a gloomy corpse
dead but for one black sulphurous vein?)

غيِّبِيني في بياضٍ صامتِ ٱلأمواجِ

فيضي يا ليالي ٱلثلجِ والغربةِ

فيضي يا ليالي

وٱمسحي ظلي وآثار نعالي ،

إمسحي برقاً أداريهِ ،

أداري حيَّةً تزهرُ في جرحي وترغي

شَرَرَ ٱلأسلاك في صدغيَّ

من صدغٍ لصدغٍ ،

VIII. Lazarus' Wife Years Later

Lose me in a whiteness of mute waves
and overflow ye nights of snow, of exile;
sweep down, wipe out my shadow and the trails   160
I leave behind; pluck out the lightning bolt
I nurtured once.
Destroy the snake that flowered in my wounds.
A raging current sparks along my face.

إمسحي ٱلخصبَ ٱلذي يُنبتُ

في ٱلسنبلِ أضراس ٱلجراد

إمسحيه ثمراً من سُمرةِ

ٱلشمس على طعم ٱلرمادْ ،

إمسحي ٱلميتَ ٱلذي ما برحتْ

تخضرُّ فيه لحيةٌ ، فخذٌ ، وأمعاءٌ تطولُ ،

جاعت ٱلأرضُ إلى شلالِ أدغالٍ

من ٱلفرسانِ ، فرسانِ ٱلمغولْ ،

هيكلٌ يركع في ٱلنارِ

تئنُّ ٱلكتبُ ٱلصفراءُ تنحل دخاناً

في حُداءاتِ ٱلخيولْ .

Wipe out fertility that breeds in stalks   165
the jaws of locust, and disintegrate
the tender glowing fruit to bitter ashes.
Wipe out the corpse in whom a greening beard
and thigh still sprout, in whom the innards lengthen.
The earth is pining for a brute cascade   170
of Mongol horsemen.
A temple on its knees in Mongol flames
and yellowing pages, murmuring, turn to smoke
amidst the whinnies of their steeds.

٩ ــ انهيار

إمسحي أَلبرق ، أمسحي أَلميتَ
أمسحي أَلخصبَ أَلذي ينبتُ في أَلسنبلِ
أضراس أَلجرادْ ،
أيّ نعشٍ باردٍ يعرقُ
في حمى أَلسهادْ
وصدى يفرش عينيَّ

IX. Collapse

Eradicate the lightning and the corpse,   175
blast the fertility that breeds
jaws of locust in wheatstalks.
What night-cold coffin sweats amidst
the fevers of insomnia:
What distant echo drapes my eyes   180

بأقمار السواد ؛

كيف كانت تنحر الدرب ُ

وفي الدرب تذوب

كيف كانت تتمطَّى الأرض ُ

تجري تحت أقدامي الدروب ْ

تلتقي في خندقٍ يمخره الوهج ُ

وإيقاعُ القطار ْ

يرسل الدخنة َ

شَعراً مُعوِلاً عبر القفار ْ ،

with moons of blackness:
how often did the road sail forth
evaporating into unseen roads:
how often the earth yawned and stretched
and sped the roads beneath my feet   185
to dwindle into barren ruts
scorched by the blazing light and by
the rhythm of the racing train,
wafting its smoke like wailing hair
across the bleak expanse.   190

أترى مرَّتْ وما مرَّتْ

على جسمي دواليب اَلقطارْ

لم أزلْ أسمعُ

في مجرى شرايبني دبيبَة

أَلدواليب اَلدواليب اَلرهيبَة

.

غيِّبيني وأمسحي ذاكرتي ، فيضي

ليالي اَلثلج في اَلأَرض اَلغريبَةْ ،

عربةُ اَلثلج وموت اَلدربِ

وَاَلجدرانِ في اَلأَرض اَلغريبه

And could it be that it has passed,
yet hasn't passed, across my flesh?
I still can hear it in my veins,
the horrible wheels, the horrible wheels.

* * *

Lose me, wipe out my memory,   195
overflow, ye snowy nights,
upon the land of banishment
ye nights, the death of road and walls
which mark the foreign land.

سوف أحكي

وأعرّي جوعَ صحرائي وعاري

سوف أحكي

قبل أن يطردَهُ ديكُ الَصباحْ

وتملَّ القيد والَمعلفَ

أفراسُ الَرياحْ :

جئتني اَلليلة ممسوحاً رماديّاً ،

وطيفاً يتراءى عبر وهجِ اَلحسّ

X. The Nazarene Appears to Lazarus' Wife

I will speak up and strip   200
the hunger of my desert and my shame
I will speak up before
the morning cock chases the ghost away,
before the horses of the wind
forsake their pasture and their reins: 205
you came tonight, a grey anointed ghost
looming, at times within the blaze of sense,

حيناً ويتيمْ

كنتَ طيفاً قبل ان يتصدَّكَ

ٱلقبر ٱلسفيهْ

عبثاً لن أدفع ٱلإصبعَ

في فجوة جرح تدَّعيهْ

.. إِن تكن جوعانَ حدِّقْ ..

ما غريبٌ أن يجوعَ ٱلطيفُ ،

أن تكسر كفَّاهُ ٱلرغيفْ

أسهر ٱلليلَ أعِدُّ الزادَ

للموتى ٱلطيوفْ ،

قُرِعَ ٱلناقوس والتمَّ ٱلضيوفْ

and vanishing at times beyond the blaze.
You were a ghost before the scurrilous grave
had sucked you dry within its vaulted walls.   210
I'll never poke my fingers in that wound.
If you are hungry, gaze!
It is not strange for ghosts to lust for food,
nor is it strange for them to break the bread.
I spend the night preparing food for ghosts.   215
The bell has rung, the guests assemble.

يـوم أنـتِ مريمٌ ، يوم تداعَتْ

زحفت تلهث في حمّى اَلبوارْ

وأزاحت عن رياحِ اَلجوعِ

في أدغالها صمتَ اَلجدارْ

وسواقي شَعْرها

أنحلَّت على رجليكَ جمراً وبهارْ

لم يعكّر صحو عينيك اَلتّياعُ

XI. The Magdalene

The day that Mary moaned, the day she crept
and crumbled, panted in her fervent wastes,
and in her jungles freed the winds of lust
from the fetters of their stony calm,   220
and when the floodgates of her hair broke open
at your feet, embers and condiment,
the clearness in your eyes remained unstirred

اَلسوطِ وٱلحيّةِ
في صلب ٱلذَكَرْ
مرَّ في ٱلصحو ملاكٌ
وٱنطوى يدمع في ظل ٱلقَمَرْ
حيث لا يُرعد جوعُ مارج بٱلزفرات

كنتَ طيفاً قمرّياً
وإلهـاً قمري
كنتَ ثوباً غائماً
يعبق بٱلضوءِ ٱلطري
يتمشى في جروح ٱلمَريمات .

by blaze of whip or snake within your sex;
an angel passed through the transparent calm,   225
and then withdrew into the shadow of the moon
to shed its tranquil tears,
where peals of hunger are inaudible.

* * *

You were a lunar ghost, a lunar god,
a cloth of clouds, hiding in mellow light   230
sauntering through the wounds of Marys.

١٢ – تنّين صريع

تنطوي صحراءُ ساقيَّ على
غصات شمسٍ تتلوّى
في ظلامٍ حَجَري
تمخر اَلغصاتُ في ساقيَّ
أليافَ اَلخلايا واَلجذورْ ،
أَلدخان اَلموحل اَلمحرورُ
يجري من غصوني وثماري

XII. A Slain Dragon

The desert of my thighs entombs the moans
of a squirming sun submerged in stony gloom;
the throes which plough my cloven length invade
each longing fibre of my rooted cells.   235
The murky smoke pours from my boughs, my fruits,

في أهازيج اَلبَراري
ويدوِّي في بخور اَلصلواتْ
يرتعي جلجلة اَلصلبِ
ويرمي في جروح اَلناصري
وجروحِ اَلمريماتْ
حسرةَ اَلانثى تشهَّتْ في اَلسريرْ
مهَّدَتْ صهوةَ نَهدَيها
تهاوت زورقاً يلهث في شط اَلهجيرْ
خلف بعلٍ لا يجير ،
من بهار اَلهند واَلفلفلِ

across the carnival clamor of the plains,
and echoes in the incense of the Mass,
grazes the hills of Golgotha
and hurls into the wounds of Marys,   240
into the wounds of Christ, the woman's pain,
pining in a lonely bed,
stroking her anxious breasts
and falling breathless on the scorching shore
after a rigid Baal, unmindful, merciless.   245
From Indian cinnamon and condiment

قطَّرتُ رحيقَهْ

في مروج ٱلجمر مرَّغتُ عروقَهْ

كان عبر ٱلسَّأم ٱلمحمومِ

يمتدُّ ٱلصقيعْ

ميِّتاً خلَّفتهُ في ٱلدارِ

تنِّيناً صريعْ

يعصر ٱللذة من جسم طريٍّ

ويروِّي شهوة ٱلموت وغلَّهْ

ليس يشتفّ سوى ٱلعهرِ

متى ٱنحرَّت له ٱلجنَّاتُ

في أعضاءِ طفلَهْ .

I have distilled the essence for his wine,
and in the glowing embers of my fields
I rubbed his dormant veins,
and yet across the heat of captive lust   250
the cold and frost had taken root.
I left him home, a slain dragon, dead,
extorting pleasure still from tender flesh,
and slaking in his lust a thirst for death.
He yearned for sheer perversion, to roam   255
the verdant fields of dainty virgin limbs.

كان في هوّة عينيهِ

صدى جنٌّ يغني اَلدرُّ واليَاقوتَ

في قاع اَلبحارْ

وفمُ اَلأُفعى متى ينشقُّ

عن وردٍ وتغريدٍ وَحبٌّ

للعصافير اَلصغارْ

In the abysmal darkness of his eyes
were echoes of the songs of emeralds,
sung by the genie deep within sea beds;
there too the subtle snake's inviting mouth   260
allured the birds with roses, seeds and songs.*

---

*According to Lebanese folklore there are snakes which prey on birds
by singing and holding seeds on their tongues.

ميتاً كان َ ،

وأدري كيف يزهو ميّتُ

يزهو يرشُّ الَضحِك المزهرَ

في جوٌّ الَوليمَة

لذةُ الَجلاد تنصبُّ على الَكأسِ

متى ما طالعته من خبايا

الَكأس أشباحُ الَجريمَة :

« جسد رصَّعه الَسوطُ وحمرُّ الَحديدْ

« بالَورود الَسود والَحمرِ

« وغدرانِ الَصديدْ

« ومحالُ يحتمي بالَموتِ

XIII. The Hangman's Pleasure

He has been dead, and I know how a corpse
can swell and strut, gilded in arrogance,
how he can, in the banquet's festive air,
scatter his laughter all around.   265
The hangman's pleasure overflows the cup,
and in its depths appear the ghosts of crime:
"A body lashed by whip and glowing steel,
with blossoming wounds of purple, flowing pus.
In vain the body cries for death   270

« من قصف الرعود

« يتهادى في صدى أشرعةٍ بيضا

« وموجاتٍ رحيمَة

« طَرَبي للكافرِ المخذولِ يَنحلُّ

« ويجري في المجاريرِ الوخيمَة

« سوف لن يرجع في الرِّيحِ

« ولن يضرب صمت البابِ بعد البابِ

« يستصرخُ ، يستسقي الدماء

« يزعج السمَّار في شجوِ المساء

« سوف لن يحكي : رفاقُ العمرِ

« غربانُ الضميرِ

« وجواسيس السفيرْ .

to keep it from the thunderous blows.
In vain it strolls upon the clement waves
or in the echoes of slapping sails.
And I will then rejoice when I behold
the vanquished blasphemer collapse   275
and flow in gutters with the filth.
No more will tempests blow him back,
nor will he pound upon the calm of doors,
nor call out loud for vengeance, thirst for blood,
disturb the revellers in their evening song;   280
nor will he ramble on about:
'friends of my youth,' 'ravens of remorse,'
or 'creeping spies of the ambassador.' "

١٤ – الجيب السحري

غيِّيني وآمسحي ظلِّي
وآثارَ نعالي .
يا ليالي آلثلج ، فيضي يا ليالي ،
إمسحي ظلِّي أنا آلأُنثى
تشهَّتْ في آلسرير ْ
خلف بعلٍ لا يجيرْ

XIV. The Magic Pouch

Lose me, wipe out my shadow and the trails
I leave behind, and overflow ye snowy nights;   285
wipe out the shadow of the Eve in me,
the woman pining in a lonely bed
after a rigid Baal, unmindful, merciless,

مارداً عاينتهُ يطلعُ
من جيب السَّفير°
وأميراً يتألَّه°
صدى السيف وما أمطر من صبحٍ
مدى الأردنِّ والكنجِ ودجلَةَ ،
عامريّاً يتولَّهُ
يعصر اللذة من جسمٍ طريٌّ
ويروِّي شهوة الموت وغلَّهُ

after a lurking giant coming forth
out of the pouch of the Ambassador,   290
after a prince who deifies himself—
The sword has rusted; no morning rain has come
to bless the Jordan, Tigris, Ganges banks—
after an Amerite* lost in the throes of love,
extorting pleasure still from tender flesh   295
and slaking in his lust a thirst for death.

---

*The reference is to Qais ibn al-Mulawwah, a pre-Islamic legendary
figure now proverbial as the man crazed by love.

غيِّبيني وَامسحي ظلِّي

وَآثار نعالي

يا ليالي اَلثلج ، فيضي يا ليالي ،

إمسحي ظلي أنا اَلانثى

بكتْ صلَّت وصلَّتْ ،

ما ترى تُغني دموعي وَاَلصلاةْ

لإلهٍ قمريٌّ ولِطيف قمري

يتخفَّى في اَلغيوم اَلزرقِ

في اَلضوءِ اَلطري

حيث لا يُرعد جوع مارج بِاَلزفراتْ

XV. The Lunar God

Lose me, wipe out my shadow and the trails
I leave behind, and overflow ye snowy nights.
Wipe out the shadow of the Eve in me,
a woman who has prayed and prayed in vain.   300
How would my supplications and my tears
affect a lunar god, a lunar ghost,
hiding in mellow light behind blue clouds
where peals of hunger are inaudible.

١٦ ـ غربة النوم

ولماذا يا بياضَ ٱلثلجِ
لا تنهلُّ في غربة نومي
مثلما تنهلُّ في ٱلأَرض ٱلغَرِيبَةْ ،
غربة ٱلنوم رهيبَةْ
لا مصابيحُ ، ولا حراسُ ليلٍ ، لا نجومْ
غيرُ جوع ٱلريح وٱلجدرانُ تهوي
وبروقٌ في دمي تزرعُها شمسُ ٱلجحيمْ ،
عَصَبٌ يصهل في غيبوبة ٱلصحرا

XVI. The Exile of Sleep

And why won't you, o whiteness of the snow,
fall down upon the exile of my sleep
just as you fall upon the foreign land?
How horrible, the exile of my sleep:
No street lights and no night guards and no stars:
only the toppling walls in hungry gales,
only the lightning in my blood,
planted and rooted by the sun of hell,
only a nerve neighing in desert calm

305

310

161

وحمّى خَدَري

طالما أستسلمتُ في غربة نومي

لغريبٍ بربري

يتعالى أخضر ٱلأعضاء

من وهجٍ حبيسٍ في ٱلظلام ٱلحجري

•

رحمةٌ .. وٱلمجد لله ٱلرحومْ

غربة ٱلنوم جحيمٌ لا تدومْ

and in the fever of my drowsiness.
How often have I yielded in my sleep   315
to a barbaric stranger with green limbs
rising from the madding glowing blaze
of light imprisoned in the stony gloom

* * *

Mercy, and glory be to the forgiving God,
the exile of my sleep is hell; it cannot last.   320

١٧ ــ جوع المجامر

ألحواسُّ ألخمسُ فوَهاتُ مجامرْ

تشتهي طعم ألدواهي وألخرابْ

تشتهي طعمَ دمي

طعمَ ألترابْ

ينطوي جسمي على جسمي

ويلتفُّ دوائرُ

ثمَّ ينحلُّ لأجسامٍ

تَمحّيها وتبنيها ألظنون :

في ضباب ألحلمِ

جسمٌ شاحب يطفو على نهرٍ حزينْ

XVII. The Hunger of Braziers

The senses are the mouths of braziers,
thirsting for apocalyptic ruin,
desiring the taste of my blood,
the relish of the dry and dusty earth.
My body folds, writhes around itself;   325
it takes on various forms
constructed and erased by whims of thought:

In the fog of dreams, a yellow shape
floats on the surface of a doleful stream,

جبهةٌ يغسلها ظلُّ شعاعْ
ويوشِّي في جبال ٱلليلِ
أطرافَ ٱلشراعْ

وهج نعليَّ
يغنِّي ويغنِّي ويغاويهِ ٱلجنونْ
مسرحي ٱلأرضُ
متى يمتصُّها ليلُ ٱلسكون ،
ويغنِّي صحوُ مرآتي ٱلرفيقَةْ :
ثوبَ عرسي ، وغلالاتي ونهدِي وبريقَةْ ،

wearing a brow washed by the shade of light   330
that, in the mountains of the gloom at night,
trims and adorns the edges of a sail.

The dazzling glow that issues from my soles
revels in songs and is by folly lured;
the whole earth is my stage when it is sucked   335
and lost in night of overwhelming calm;
and when the clearness of my mirror sings,
"my wedding dress, my veils, my glowing breasts."

حلوة سمرا رشيقَة

تمرج الدرب إلى بابي غريقَة

في أهازيج الصبايا والطيوبْ

عاد لي من غربة الموت الحبيبْ

حلوة سمرا رشيقَة

خدعة المرآة ، ربَّاهُ ، وتمويهُ العيونْ

إنَّ لي جسماً

تُمحِّيه وتبنيه الظنون .

A graceful, darksome girl. The road exults
and surges to my door immersed in scent   340
and in the songs of cheerful, youthful girls.
My love came back from the exile of death.

A graceful, darksome girl, the eye's mirage,
O God: and mirrors' fraudulent pretense.
I have a body built and then erased   345
by quick presumptions and by whims of thought.

أنطوي في حفرتي

أفعى عتيقةَ

تنسج القمصانَ

من أبخرةِ ٱلكبريت ، من وهج ٱلنيوبْ

لحبيب عاد من حفرتهِ

مَيتاً كئيبْ

لحبيب ينزف ٱلكبريتَ

مسودَّ ٱللهيبْ .

*

(كنت أسترحم عينيهِ)

(وفي عَينيَّ عارُ أمرأةٍ)

(أنتْ ، تعرَّتْ لغريبْ)

(عاد من حفرته ميتاً كئيبْ)

I shrink into my pit, an ancient snake
weaving the sulphur fumes, a glow of fangs,   350
shirts for my love who came from his exile
a gloomy corpse, bleeding black sulphur flames.

* * *

(I pled with him; I begged his distant eyes,
to pity in my eyes a woman's shame,
who moaned, undressed before a stranger's eyes.
He came back from his pit a gloomy corpse.)

Plurals in Singular Form:
The Transformations of "Lazarus 1962"

As we move from discussions of the previous two poems, "The Cave" and "The Genie of the Beach," it would not be difficult to look back at them as overtures to the poem translated here. In both of them the condition of exile is so drastically emphasized that its social contexts (present, but intuited, implied as the source of that exile) are felt as secondary. The focus is on the act of perception, on poetic creation as a process. "Lazarus," however, is less distanced esthetically, more direct, open, personal: its shifting, fragmented narrative texture resembles that of the two previous poems, but it unfolds on a level of greater referentiality, bringing to the foreground the social and political dimensions which were latent there. Two scenarios worked out in "Lazarus" were implicitly avoided in the other *Bayadir* poems: Lazarus is a man of action, thus opposed to the poet of "The Cave"; Lazarus's wife is a victim within society, thus an alternative to the gypsy, whose power is her resistance in exile and reclusion.

"Lazarus 1962" has been called prophetic, an anticipation of the 1967 Arab defeat which other poets dealt with retrospectively,[1] as if Hawi had heard that note of despair before it sounded in fact. What permits this sense of prophecy is a generalizing process characteristic of Hawi, a studied refusal to stop at particular detail.[2] Hawi is not a poet of occasions: occasions are strongly felt in his poetry but they are not themselves its materials. We can take the figure of

Sindbad from an earlier poem as an exemplification of Hawi's
strategy as a poet:

> And now that the vision sings in my blood
> with lightning's twitch, with purity of dawn,
> with instinct of the birds which sniff
> intentions hidden in the woods and winds
> and feel the seasons in the womb of time
> before the seasons spring to life.
> The vision boils and the day will come
> when I shall say what I shall say.
>   (Al-rihla al-thamina)[3]

Hawi's particular angle of vision as an observer of society
characteristically focuses on mythical figures—his Sindbad,
his Lazarus, and the unnamed (and unvisualizable?) hero in
Al-Ra'd al-jarih ("The Wounded Thunder," 1979). Firmly
rooted in the consciousness of Arab readers of poetry, they
nevertheless go through a process of defamiliarization, a
process of growth at once ahistorical and particular.

"Lazarus 1962," like the two poems which precede it in
Bayadir al-ju', is composed of soliloquies, but soliloquies by
more than one speaker. We hear not only Lazarus and his wife
but a Hawi figure in the synoptic introduction, speaking in the
first person as a commenting observer. In the introduction to
"The Genie of the Beach," we argued, the poet struggles to
control an entity that has been let loose, a character who has
developed her own consistency beyond the poet's total
control. The Hawi of that introduction is the poet materialized
as critic on the horizon of his own poem; the Hawi who
introduces "Lazarus 1962" speaks with a wholly different kind
of authority, almost as a character in the poem, a speaker who
indicates a present world: "And here is your wife. . .".
Compare kuntu shahidan, "I was a witness," in the
concluding sentence of the synopsis in "Lazarus 1962," with
the acts of seeing which open "The Cave," the hard-edged
distancing of the one and the defiant gesture of presence in the
former. "Lazarus 1962" is unmistakably a poem about
experience, to use Hawi's privileged term, about mu'anat—
not strictly the mu'anat which goes on between poet and text
but the experiences of the shared world. This is one source of

the sense of familiarity which sets this poem apart from its predecessors.

A second source of that familiarity is Hawi's use of allusion. As in "Sindbad's Eighth Voyage" (In *Al-Nay wa al-rih*, 1961), the central figure is someone we know before we have read the poem, about whom we have associations even if we have not read the *Arabian Nights* or the New Testament. Lazarus means resurrection as Sindbad means the Odyssean, Faustian quest for knowledge and experience. This minimal familiarity, as Hawi has said,[4] is essential for enabling the reader to identify pre-critically, perhaps emotionally, with the poet's intention. For a poet with Hawi's penchant for compact expression, glancing allusion and ellipsis, the reader's prior associations can be used to minimize the use of narration and explicit transition in general. Symbolic art, Hawi has said is distinct from storytelling or portraiture. "The symbol helps the poet to eliminate narration, interpretation and direct statement."[5] Like the events described in "The Cave," the episodes alluded to in the soliloquies of "Lazarus" are discontinuous, stages in a process in which cause and effect, even sequence, have been minimalized. Unlike the events of "The Cave," the legendary, familiar mythic elements of "Lazarus" make the text transparent. The vehicle: A New Testament narrative; the tenor: tendencies in contemporary Arab society and civilization. The former Hawi calls intellectual, the second, emotional.[6] The Bible narrative distances, magnifies, gives shape to experience which otherwise might tempt the poet to naive and uncontrolled rage.[7] Emotion seeks a specific target. The legend evades that easy release. It puts it on an intellectual level. It concretizes, but at a level of abstraction higher than that which would point out specific persons, specific institutions or issues. We locate the tenor of the poem not in a critique of Arab leaders since 1952, not even necessarily in the Arab world, but in general processes in the chemistry of power and its corruption which can be used as models for recent Arab history. The confrontation between the priest and gypsy in "The Genie of the Beach" we interpreted as a temptation of univalent meaning, of naive referentiality. Here we are as close as Hawi comes to a social manifesto, and the Lazarus pattern acts as a limit to the contraction of meaning. (This limit supports the structure at a level of generality which isolates synchronic processes in history: it is in this mirror that he sees the future.)

The opening three vignettes are spoken by a Lazarus, not exactly the Lazarus we infer from the New Testament story (nor the existential Lazarus of Kazantzakis's novel *The Last Temptation of Christ*, whose function is primarily to question the promise of another world), but a lazarus who yearns to be reburied. Sections two and three provide a kind of background to that death-wish; they fill in what we might call earlier stages of the argument. The opening section is the hypothesis, the *quod est demonstrandum*; what follows constitutes the *causae rei*. Its mode is hyperbole. Its celestial landscape marks a point as far as the poem shows us from a specific social setting—the opposite pole of referentiality, and the scope of that scene, the list of entities he wishes himself isolated from, expands unpredictably. The pit (*hufra*) without a bottom (*qaʻ*) is already an exaggeration pointing in the direction of the surprises which follow. In line three the pit goes through the earth and out the other side, continuing across the solar system to a realm beyond vision, into darkness (lines 4-5), and then (in a move which translates the hyperbole back into human terms) a realm beyond sound ("No echo. . ."), thus beyond communication. The word *madar*, "orbit," is the site of another sudden expansion of scope. Having pushed through the circumference of the earth we expect the next step in the expanding reference to be the next largest circle, the earth's orbit. Instead it is the orbit of the sun through the galaxy, as if the solar system were itself too domestic and circumscribed a locality. Meanwhile *madar* joins other words which—though not of the same morpho-syntactic form—resemble it: *haffar*, "gravedigger" and *qarar*, "bottom" (but also with a hint of the coming political context, "decision," "stability"; *dar al-qarar*, "the hereafter," "the world to come"). In line four we get its anagram, *ramad*, "ash," in the phrase *laylan min ramadin*, "a night (made) of ashes." Ashes are a common image for inconstancy, a favored term in contemporary Arabic poetry, and particularly in Hawi,[8] a substance that crumbles and drifts away at the mercy of the shifting air. The image of the sun's orbit, already an icon of the intangible—simply a track along which a concrete entity moves—becomes in contrast to the ash a vision of substantiality (since the orbit, though non-material, is fixed, bounded, predictable and symmetrical in shape). On the level of the signifier, the economy of expression which conveys that leap simply by rearrangement of the three consonants is remarkable.

The wish of the opening is a communication act which turns on itself: the imperative '*ammiq*, "deepen," involves not the muse, as the accustomed epic aid to eloquence, but a power who buries, conceals, hides, a *haffar*, a gravedigger, thus depicting a sensibility which could be called anti-epic. The initiating desire is not for entombment as enclosure and solidity, but for loss and exile, for entombment as freedom, entombment in a pit which is bottomless, *li-qa'in la qarar*, thus not enclosing. The defamiliarization of the Bible narrative is present in the unstated, in absences so subtle they may pass unnoticed. The metaphysical questions of death as non-being, versus a continuance after death are not broached.

We are signaled immediately that the tenor of the poem will be diverted from the field of reference normally seen in the Biblical vehicle. The issues in the Bible story as it is traditionally interpreted are being and non-being, life and death; the paradoxes of Lazarus's speech (his need to be buried or relocated in sites of increasing deathliness, increasing absence, as if death were a state subject to degree) nudge us into the social issue, but mutely. Life we take as a reformed society, as in Spengler's biological metaphor, and death we take as a figure for decadence and corruption, an opposition whose specific reference might be the glorious Arab past versus post-Mongol decadence. The equivalent of resurrection in the Bible story, what Hawi terms in his prose synopsis "life and death in life" (*al-hayat wa al-mawt fi al-hayat*), is the continued absence of unifying values in Arab society, decadence in the guise of renaissance during the age of Arab revolution.

Stated in other terms, "Lazarus 1962" delineates a vision of history which grounds personal salvation (in secular terms, fulfillment) in a cultural framework. There are two stages in this vision. The first is a widening of the scope of historical reference, a vision of a Mediterranean culture defined through archaic myth, making the present transparent (in the generalizing process we spoke of above), therefore no longer

bound by the historical restrictions of a post-colonial Arab
world. This widening of scope he shares with the
Tammuziyyun poets (Badr Shakir al-Sayyab, 'Abd al-Mu'ti
Hijazi, Yusuf al-Khal, the early Adonis); it is an imagery with
analogues in the writings of Antun Sa'ada, founder of the Parti
Populaire Syrien (Al-Hizb al-Suri al-Qawmi al-'Ijtima'i),
whose concept of a Greater Syria rested on a definition of a
coherent secular culture in the eastern Mediterranean and the
fertile crescent which has survived millennia of demographic
change. In Antun Sa'ada's writings this coherence is latent,
potential, unacknowledged unless it is based on genuine,
authentic human values, a sense of individual commitment
(manaqib) which links individual and culture in an act of will.
This distinction brings us to the second stage which becomes
visible in part VI. It is this virtue, this manaqibiyya, whose
absence is reponsible figuratively for the vanquishing of St.
George (al-Khidr—see note to Part VI of the translation). The
hero's failure figures a loss of will, of commitment, on the part
of leaders who grew out of such movements, a failure of will
which results in a mechanical, unresponsive reaction to
political problems. Thus the dragon is something mechanical,
a machine, and the vanquishing of St. George becomes a way
of suggesting that Lazarus as a political actor has taken on the
rhythms of an automaton, and the jumpy, fragmented
rhythms of the narration work to the same effect.

It is not enough to speak of gaps in the narrative coherence
of the poem; there are also jumps from one narrative to
another. We might call them successive subversions which
erode the mythical and biblical references. The vehicle of the
poem gives us our language, our distance from the specifics of
history, but it would not be a vehicle if it did not at some points
become transparent, giving way to specificity of a different
kind, the tenor of the poem indicated by the date affixed to the
title, which materializes in fragments. In the space between a
Bible story which keeps disappearing and a documentary of
Arab society, which crops up only in glimpses, but which gains
intensity as the poem proceeds, we feel a parallel subversion
of time and space. The seeming anachronisms—the fashion
magazines (nutafun min suhufi al-azyai': line 139 of the
translation), the train (188ff), are breaches in the wall of the
legend, and even the references to the Mongols (170-174) and

the story of St. George in parts six and seven are anachronisms. In the first three parts, Lazarus's monologue, "the multitudes," "the flaming wheels," "the ghouls" who walk the street, are markers of the social setting. A line like "What has been is, what is has been unchanged" (31), glaringly inappropriate to the distinction between life and death, is another.

Among the subversions of the scriptures are the ascription of the conversation with Jesus from John II.20-23 and 11.32 to Mary instead of Martha. The substitution has the appearance of a meaningful one, but we cannot fully account for it. Is it simply that Mary is a name of greater resonance, designating as it does two other Biblical figures—one a famous virgin, the other a famous prostitute—thus introducing a sexual register played upon repeatedly in the poem? The other alteration is simply the addition of Lazarus's wife to the cast, unmentioned in the Bible narrative. Her story is of course the gradual assimilation of Lazarus's attributes to her, as she metamorphoses, like him, from a positive figure, to a victim of distorted vision, to an agent of aggression—a transformation which is, as we shall see momentarily, not limited to her. In part four she has already noticed a change in her returned spouse, a change introduced here in the refrain (lines 71-75) which will recur to characterize their relationship of bondage:

> I pled with him, I begged his distant eyes
> to pity in my eyes a woman's shame,
> who moaned, undressed before a stranger's eyes.
> Why did he leave his pit, a gloomy corpse,
> dead but for one black sulphurous vein?

In part five she denies to her neighbor what she has just said, privately, to us, in a speech which pretends that his return has brought happiness to the household. The rhythm of part five changes abruptly from the somber epic (or anti-epic) pace of the opening sections to a light, staccato rhythm that camouflages the meter. (The flexibility with which Hawi produces variations within the *ramal* meter—expanding the basic foot *fa'ilatun* [u-uu] by increasing the proportion of open syllables to produce extraordinary changes of mood—is one

of his great contributions to modern Arabic poetry.) In part
six she recounts his coming to her in the days before his death,
"vanquished, wounded and incurable" but human, preferable
to his revivified self. It is here that we read the most nearly
direct account of his fall, when she quotes him in the role of St.
George, telling their story in displaced form. Here St. George
is vanquished by his dragon (118-29), and the updated,
mechanized nature of the dragon, which we referred to in
political terms above, is also a vision of technological pro-
gress, of nineteenth-century optimism. Hawi's distrust of
nineteenth-century idealism, as it is found in the naive
affirmations of popular poetry at all levels, is an attempt to
construct a world view which allows no traces of the facile
confidence in indefinite progress and the victory of virtue. It
becomes an attempt to visualize a world in which vice is
perfectly capable of a total, universal victory. (We know from
part twelve, perhaps more clearly, what the reader has already
intuited, that St. George becomes his own dragon. When this
happens, pronouns cease to function in the anticipated ways,
resulting in a dilemma like that we described in our
interpretation of "The Cave": the specular undermining of
shifters. But here the linguistic ambiguity has a political
dimension: the attenuation of distinct identity. Hawi's
generalizing process, which keeps the figure rather than a
particular interpretation of it in the foreground, works to echo
the erosion of identity which afflicts the public man, whose self
becomes the oversimplified persona developed to meet a
public, and once simplified reduplicates itself in its followers—
the familiar mechanism of conformity in a repressive society,
the phenomenon from which the narrator recoils in horror at
the close of the introduction.)

Stories of dragon-killers conventionally end in weddings. In
part seven the narrative continues with a wedding of sorts, but
it is a wedding of death. St. George, or Lazarus, is an
experienced hero who realizes what the causes of his defeat
are, and is resigned to it, in fact too resigned. It may be that he
is alone at this point in recognizing that he has been defeated
at all. The wedding bells (which seem to suggest the praises of
history) are still ringing (146-47), but he ignores them. In
section eight Lazarus's wife repeats in slightly altered form the
response to defeat which he began in section one. She too

wishes for burial and oblivion (in the "whiteness of mute waves"—line 158) and sees him in his aspect of walking corpse — vision of a decadent Arab world which is masquerading as a newly born society. At this point the historical dialogue invades the vehicle explicitly. Two images radiate outward through the poem with particular power here, one explicit and relatively arcane, both underlining her wish for non-being. The first is the invasion of the Mongols, seen as a kind of sexual aggression. Meanwhile the perverse fertility which disintegrates "the tender glowing fruit to bitter ashes" (167) alludes to the fruit of Sodom image in the writings of the historian Josephus. Traveling by the Dead Sea, he observes in *The Jewish War* (4.8.4.), "Still . . . may one see ashes reproduced in the fruits, which from their outward appearance would be thought edible, but on being plucked with the hand dissolve into smoke and ashes."[9] In itself it is not an allusion of great moment, but the concept by which earthly sin encroaches on the forms of the natural world, culture altering nature, appealed strongly to renaissance scholiasts and generated the scene in *Paradise Lost* where Satan, celebrating the fall of Eve and Adam, is transformed into a serpent and climbs an image of the tree of knowledge which has sprung up before him and his accomplices:

> and up the Trees
> Climbing, sat thicker than the snaky locks
> That curl'd *Megaera:* greedily they pluck'd
> The Fruitage fair to sight, like that which grew
> Near that bituminous Lake where Sodom flam'd;
> This more delusive, not the touch, but taste
> Deceiv'd; they fondly thinking to allay
> Thir appetite with gust, instead of Fruit
> Chew'd bitter Ashes, which th'offended taste
> With spattering noise rejected: oft they assay'd
> Hunger and thirst constraining, drugg'd as oft,
> With hatefullest disrelish writh'd thir jaws
> With soot and cinders fill'd; so oft they fell
> Into the same illusion . . .[10]   (X. 558-71)

This passage, which combines the Sodom allusion with motifs of a marriage fallen on hard times and transformation into

snakes (Lazarus is seen as a snake at 260; his wife becomes
one at 347), is likely to have occurred to Hawi in the
composition of this poem. (Hawi's knowledge of English
poetry is formidable; we hear Miltonic echoes in this poem as
we hear allusions to Yeats at the close of "The Cave.") The
thrust of the allusion here is to amplify parallels between
husband and wife. What Lazarus expressed in the language of
astronomy in part one his wife describes in terms of
vegetation. By virtue of the Josephus image the result is the
same, ashes (the ashes of the glowing fruit leading us back to
the "night of ashes" in line 4). In part nine her condition is like
his, one of numbness, a state of vertigo so complete that there
is no point of reference from which to measure it:

> . . . how often did the road sail forth
> evaporating into unseen roads:
> how often the earth yawned and stretched
> and sped the roads beneath my feet
> to dwindle into barren ruts
> scorched by the blazing light and by
> the rhythm of the racing train,
> wafting its smoke like wailing hair
> across the bleak expanse.

In an image which acts as a sinister inversion to the beckoning
road in the closing moment of "The Cave," we have here a
road whose motion is dizzying, which becomes in turn desert
ruts and, in another manifestation of technological progress
like the dragon which becomes one with St. George, a train.
(The Arabic term qitar, like the English word, suggests a string
or procession of like objects, thus a hint of formlessness, "A
nightmare shape if shape it might be called/That shape had
none," 122-23, which made the dragon a source of terror.) The
wheels of the train work as an inversion of the theme of vast
circles in the orbits of the opening. If Lazarus was trying to lose
himself in the vastness of the universe, his wife loses herself in
the reaches of her inner being, and the result is a kind of terror
at her own numbness, as she attempts to distinguish the
reality of being run across by the passing train from her
fantasy of it. The centrality of the section is underlined by its
title, inhiyar, "collapse, breakdown," the term used

prominently in the introduction to describe the historical moment of the poem.

In part ten the resurrection of Lazarus and the resurrection of Jesus also begin to coalesce: "I'll never poke my fingers in that wound" (211). Lazarus's wife has already occupied, and refused, the role of Doubting Thomas. (She is even more a skeptic because she refuses to test the reality.) This germinal moment is amplified in the condemnation of Jesus in section eleven. The story of Magdalene's frustration with the spiritual, anti-sensual Jesus becomes a figure for the conjugal relationship (or its absence) between Lazarus and his wife. A third level of analogy makes this a political scenario. Jesus resurrects Lazarus: Similarly Hawi suggests that the ideals which make possible the Arab reform movement are analogous to a divine power, an agent of rebirth. On the level of the figurative narrative, the two resurrected heroes exemplify contrary evasions of earthly contact: Jesus through inordinate emphasis on chastity (as a lunar god, pale and distant), Lazarus through lust, perversion and demonic charm (like the charm of the seed-bearing snake, 260-61). Corrupted sensuality, extending the Spenglerian metaphor, becomes sadism in section thirteen. In section fourteen he is both spy and rapist (295-96). This marks the end of a series of successive solidifications, where the context has narrowed to a nearly explicit condemnation of modern Arab society of that moment in history. Lazarus is momentarily assimilated to Baal, the pagan fertility god declared an invalid source of redemption in "Sindbad's Eighth Voyage."[11]

The poem's final moments are in the form of reprises; in section fifteen the wife's lyric restatement of the wish for non-being, in section sixteen the longing for a non-being more radical than that of sleep, since her sleep is the site of dreams which continue the torments of waking. The analogy between her exhortations and those of Lazarus in the opening section is so complete that it hardly matters who is speaking. (Again, "I was a witness: I saw you in the ranks of all of them.") This process continues in section seventeen to a point where transformations become evidently free-flowing, unbound by a narrative logic or a necessary link to the Bible story. It is as if an emotional energy released by the moments of direct referentiality which surfaced in parts 13 and 14 threatened to

waste the power of the poem in parochial issues; the
concluding monologue (parts fifteen through seventeen), by
retreating first within the Bible story and then within the series
of transformations Lazarus's wife imagines, draws the con-
text farther outward, away from the specific. Her trans-
formations are not unmotivated. The opening of "The
Hunger of Braziers" is another in the list of pleas for escape,
except that here we watch the escape happening:

> My body folds, writhes around itself;
> it takes on various forms
> constructed and erased by whims of thought . . .
>   (325-28)

The act of folding, intiwa', yantawi, "to fold," is at once an
expression of pain and the beginning of the transformation:
the mood of longing and vain exhortation which has
dominated the poem seems at last to have changed, and when
it does the transformations continue without a resting place.
She sees herself first as an Ophelia figure floating down a
stream, itself an image of flux. The second transformation (in
imagery reminiscent of "The Genie of the Beach") makes her
a happy, blushing bride—the one thing the poem has carefully
proven that she is not. It is a recapitulation of section five,
"Ornament," where we heard her lying to a friend, portraying
the marriage to Lazarus as a state of joy. Once more there is a
vision of a road in motion (339-40), but here it is a redemptive
motion, a dance. But it would oversimplify the situation to say
simply that lines 333-343 are an ironic reprise of part five. The
illusion in part five was outwardly directed, a construct to
meet the demands of decorum. Here the decorum is
internalized, as if now the despair had become so intense she
even attempts to fool herself. It is as if we are given a glimpse
not only of her metamorphosis but the process which leads
from a conscious pretense to a psychological necessity. And
yet it is clear that there is something in the speaking
consciousness which is not fooled, which is still aware of the
pretense. The passing observation, "the whole earth is my
stage" (335), could mean that she has become so beautiful
that everyone looks at her; it could also mean that the scene
is illusory, a creation at her disposal. "The clearness of my

mirror" (337) becomes "mirrors' fraudulent pretense" in line 344.

Hawi has always been a poet of metamorphoses, often of metamorphoses which occupy a peculiar space where figurative language and physical transformation are hard to distinguish. In Ovid's *Metamorphoses*, the classical compendium of transformations, a human typically alters into a non-human form which is the concretion of a moral state. Ovid's focus tends to be dramatic, a focus which emphasizes the physical nature of the alteration. When Cadmus becomes a snake for instance (*Metamorphoses* IV. 563 ff) we see the physical restrictions come over his human will:

> He stretched out full-length forward, felt his skin
> Harden, and scales increase, and mottled markings
> Sprinkle his blackening belly, with his legs behind him
> Drawn in, and tapering. He still had arms
> And tried to reach them forward . . .[12]

In the major passages of post-classical western culture which imitate it (*Inferno* XXV. 103-44 and *Paradise Lost* X.511-15) the emphasis is the same, on the transformation as a process. Hawi, as we noticed in "The Cave," does not work narratively; successive states coexist as if they were stations in a process which repeats, rather than a description of an individual going through the state. Northrop Frye, in an essay that compares *Finnegans Wake* with Blake's prophecies, distinguishes those projects of comparable scope by observing that Joyce's treatment of the cycles of history emphasizes their recurrence: Blake's cycles emphasize the possibility that the system can be broken in an imaginative act.[13] Hawi seems so far to side with Joyce. We tend to see his metamorphoses as events already in the past, changes which the object of change perceives in himself, belatedly ("And I've become a cave. . ." "The Cave,"line 3). In our discussion of "The Genie of the Beach" the question arose whether in fact we could consider one stage in the process as a ground-zero reality from which the rest departs. This does not mean that Hawi operates utterly outside the tradition of Ovid. In fact, the closing of the poem, so deemphasized that he seems purposely to have buried it, to make us work for its significance, is a trans-formation with a subtle and indirect reference to the *Meta-*

morphoses, though, strangely, not to one of its transfor-
mations. When Lazarus's wife in a final moment see herself as
a snake, she adds as if in passing that she is weaving a shirt.
The material from which she weaves it is fumes of sulphur,
which have also been the image used to describe Lazarus's
blood. Hercules' wife, Deianira, gives Hercules a shirt be-
cause she has been assured by the centaur Nessus that it is
a love charm to prevent his philandering. As we know, the
shirt turns to fire and grows to his flesh, and the slow death
of Hercules is one of Ovid's set pieces (IX. 157-272). Coming
as it does at the close of the poem, this is an important re-
ference; we perhaps see something different in it than Hawi
saw, but this garment which enters the text in the most
indirect way seems to be of a piece with previous images of
cloth in the divan, the shroud in "The Cave," the tents in "The
Genie of the Beach," which we took as images of the poem. A
cloth which grows painfully to the skin we may take to be an
image of a poetry whose referentiality has stretched to a
point where it threatens the esthetic coherence of the poem's
fabric.

"Lazarus 1962" is universally taken to be a pessimistic
statement.[14] Hawi himself has reacted noncommittally to that
criticism. Surely the conclusion shows us Lazarus's wife
forced into the same scenario of degradation which dragged
him from a sympathetic character to another agent of
aggression in the name of worthwhile ideals. Do we
experience her final descent as the occasion for an act of
cathartic violence, or is she simply brought down to his level?
As a narrative alone "Lazarus" bears out the pessimistic
reading of the critics, but something else has happened in
section seventeen to ameliorate that darkness and put Hawi
on the side of Blake. The mere fact that in her dark moment
Lazarus's wife is conscious of her own change adds an
increment of control to the system which itself alters it. Since
the machinery of transformation is founded on a failure of
vision, the poet's depiction works to alter the system in the act
of depicting it, and the world of identical masks we have been
taught by the introduction to see affixed to every face within
the poem becomes less important than the face of the reader,
who in recognizing it creates the possibility of resisting the
spell.

Notes

[1]See, for example, Rita 'Awad, *Usturat al-mawt wa al-inbi'ath fi al-shi'r al-'Arabi al-Hadith* (Beirut, 1978), pp. 116-117.

[2]This is perhaps with Hawi means when he says his symbols are both intellectual and emotional. See Musa Al-Sardawi, "Hadith ma'al-duktur Khalil Hawi," *Al-Adab*, 8 (July, 1963): 72.

[3]"Sindbad's Eighth Voyage," (*Diwan*, Beirut, n.d.), pp. 261-262.

[4]"Thawrat al-shi'r al-hadith fi mu'tayatiha al-asasiyya," *Al-Usbu'* al-'Arabi, 13 (November 29, 1971): 65.

[5]Sardawi, "Hadith," p. 72.

[6]Sardawi, "Hadith," p. 72.

[7]It may be difficult for western readers that what later becomes a critique of the Christian world view is also made the figure for a critique of Arab society. Westerners tend to perceive Arab and Muslim as co-terminous adjectives. For Hawi (no less Arab than Christian) the equation is not so simple.

[8]Ashes in *Nahr al ramad*, Hawi's first *diwan*, are associated with fire and resurrection.

[9]Trans. H. St. J. Thackeray (London, 1928), Vol. 3, pp. 142-45.

[10]John Milton, *Complete Poems and Major Prose*, ed. Merritt Y. Hughes (New York, 1959).

[11]Sec 9, ll 1-3, *Diwan*, p. 262.

[12]Trans. Rolfe Humphries (Ind. U.P., 1957).

[13]Northrop Frye, *Fables of Identity* (Harcourt, Brace, 1963), pp. 256-264.

[14]See, for example, Husayn Muruwwa, "Bayadir al-Ju'," in Hawi's *Diwan*, pp. 457-64.

"Ya Sabiyya"

Previously unpublished poem in Hawi's own hand

يا صبيّة

يا حبيّة !
يا حبيّة !
كيف الربيع رمادي و مضوعي
كيف الطلعت صبيّا
في حروفي و طلوعي
طلعة مرتى طريّه
و غلّت الزهر في عينيه
من هون الفـ....يه

(يا حبيّة !)
(يا حبيّة !)
و مدى الزهد جلّى
جـــد في زهوه دورن غلاله
و جبّي لهافر عمرج ته
رتقته
يسعلاه صلا له

Young Woman

Young woman
my dear
young woman,
how you have kindled
these ashes—
this frost
how you have revived the young man
in my veins,
in ardor and in tenderness,
how you have washed
the ostentation flowering in his eyes
clean of evening's terror.

And, young woman
my dear
young woman,
in the full extent
of youthful vanity
a body in its ostentation
blooms forth, without the slightest veil,
and a young man
cavorts, exulting in it
grazing to its roots
filling up on it
with guiltless abandon.

جسد دون غلاله

جسده ذاب شاطئ المدى

ومساه اللحن ما خلف المدى

ومدى الأرض وعطاء المدى

جسد دون غلاله

جسده الأرض تجلّت

هالة هفت وهاله

أشرقت درب الطلال

خلقت نقل الجبال

دفقت نقل العشية

دفقت هول الكبية

يا حبيبة !

يا حبيبة !

خليل حاوي   ١٤/٤/٨١

A body without the slightest veil
around it have melted
the mazes of space
and mazes of reflection
beyond distance
beyond yesterday's echo
beyond echo's choking.

A body without the slightest veil
around it earth self-manifests,
a halo shapes itself, repeats,
its shadow mornings forth
disrobes the weight of mountains
dismantles the weight of evening
dissolves evening's terror
young woman,
my dear
young woman
young woman.

14 April 1981
Khalil Hawi

193

Bibliography

I. Works by Khalil Hawi

A. Collections of poetry (in chronological order)

Nahr al-ramad (Beirut, 1957).
Al-Nay wa al-rih (Beirut, 1961).
Bayadir al-ju' (Beirut, 1965)
Al-Ra'd al-jarih (Beirut, 1979).
Min jahim al-kumidya (Beirut, 1979).
Diwan Khalil Hawi (Beirut, 1979).

B. Other book-length works

Al-'Aql wa al-iman bayn al-Ghazzali wa Ibn Rushd (unpublished
    M.A. thesis, American University of Beirut, 1955).
Gibran Kahlil Gibran: His Background, Character and Works
    (Beirut, 1972; 2nd ed., London, 1982).
Editor-in-Chief, *Encyclopedia of Arabic Poetry* (Beirut, 1974).

C. Poems published in periodicals (in alphabetical order)

"Asya ba'd al-jalid," *Al-Adab* 11 (November 1956): 28.
" 'Awda ila Sadum," *Al-Adab* 9 (September 1957): 12.
"Bila 'unwan," *Al-Adab* 6 (June 1957): 24.
"Da'wa qadima," *Al-Adab* 6 (June 1961): 17.
"Al-Dhura al-bayda'," *Al-Adab* 5 (May, 1955): 57.
"Fi biladihim," *Al-Adab* 2 (February 1957): 10.
"Fi ghaybat al-hulm," *Al-Adab* 2 (February, 1954): 31.
"Fi al-mathar," *Al-Adab* 6 (June 1954): 16.
"Hubb wa juljula," *Al-Adab* 3 (March 1957): 11.
" 'Ind al-bassara," *Al-Adab* 12 (December 1960): 10-11.
"Ishraq," *Al-Adab* 12 (December 1953): 14.
"Al-Jazzar," *Al-Adab* 1 (January 1959): 25.
"Jinniyyat al-shati'," *Al-Adab* 7 (July 1961): 4-5.
"Al-Jisr," *Al-Adab* 5 (May 1957): 21.

"Al-Juruh al-sud," *Al-Adab* 8 (August 1961): 21.
"Al-Kahf al-jai'," *Al-Adab* 2 (February 1962): 5.
"Al-Khudra al-tafira," *Al-Adab* 3 (March 1954): 40.
"Li'azar 1962," *Al-Adab* 6 (June 1962): 8.
"Al-Majus fi Urubba," *Al-Adab* 10 (October 1957): 12.
"Al-Nay wa rih al-sawma'a," *Al-Adab* 2 (February 1959): 10.
"Qurban al-jasad," *Al-'Urwa al-wuthqa* (December 1950): 16-17.
"Rahma mal'una," *Durub* 24 (1965): 24.
"Al-Sajin," *Shi'r* 2 (Spring 1957): 6.
"Al-Sindibad fi rihlatihi al-thamina," *Al-Adab* 5 (May 1960): 19-21.
"Wujuh al-Sindibad," *Al-Adab* 1 (January 1958): 62.
"Tab' al-qadar," "Asatin," and "Ya samra" [in the Lebanese ver-
   nacular], *Al-Udisya* (November? 1982): n.p.

D. Articles by and interviews with Khalil Hawi (in alphabetical order)

"Al-'Aql wa al-iman," *Al-Abhath* 1 (1956): 49-70.
"Al-'Aql wa al-iman fi al-hadara al-'Arabiyya," *Al-Fikr al-'Arabi al-
   mu'asir* 2 (June 1980): 32-36.
"Al-'Aql wa al-iman fi al-hadara al-gharbiyya al-haditha," *Al-Fikr
   al-'Arabi al-mu'asir* 4, 5 (August 1980): 122-127.
"Falsafat al-shi'r al-gharbi al-hadith," *Al-Adab* 3 (March 1962):
   13-18.
"Hadha al-'alam al-'Arabi," *Al-Abhath* 4 (April 1953): 557-560.
"Hal al-hadara al-'Arabiyya al-hadira fawrat yatba 'uha khumud?,"
   Wujhat nazar 8 (12 February 1975).
"Hawl diwan *Nar wa nabidh,*" *Al-Muharrir* (11 April 1968): 5.
"Al-Iman al-Sufi fi madhhab al-Ghazzali," *Al-Fikr al-'Arabi al-
   mu'asir* 8, 9 (December 1980, January 1981): 83-86.
" 'Ind sarir al-Sayyab," *Al-Adab* 2 (February 1965): 1-2.
"Interview," *Al-Tariq* 1 (January 1971): 92-96.
"Introduction," to Al-Karki, Karim, *Nar wa nabidh* (Beirut, 1968):
   7-14.
"Al-Khalq al-'udwi fi nazariyyat al-shi'r wa naqdih,' *Al-Adab* 1
   (January 1969): 18-22.
"Ma'alim al-fikr al-'Arabi: Kamal al-Yaziji," *Al-Adab* 12 (December
   1954): 36.
"Al-Nahda wa al-bahth 'an al-huwiyya," *Al-Fikr al-'Arabi al-
   mu'asir* 17 (December 1981, January 1982): 30-45.
"Notice" on the cover of 'Ataya, Shafiq, *The Earth Woman*
   (Roslyn Heights, New York, 1976).
"Al-Sha'ir 'Abd Allah Ghanim," *A'lam min al-Matn* (Beirut, 1959):
   21-25.
"Al-Shi'r al-hadith," *Al-Hikma* 2 (February 1961): 11-13, 56.

II. Works about Khalil Hawi

A. Studies and comments in books and anthologies

'Abbas, Ihsan, *Ittijahat al-shi'r al-'Arabi al-mu'asir* (Kuwait, 1978): especially 170-171, 238-250.

'Awad, Rita. *Adabuna al-hadith bayn al-ru'ya wa al-ta'bir* (Beirut, 1979): 69-172.

_____. *Usturat al-mawt wa al-inbi'ath fi al-shi'r al-'Arabi al-hadith* (Beirut, 1978): 112-133.

'Awad, Yusuf Nur. *Ruwwad al-shi'r al-hadith* (Kuwait, n.d.): 205-228.

Badawi, Mustafa. *A Critical Introduction to Modern Arabic Poetry* (London, 1975): 245-250.

Ghanimi, Muhammad H. *Al-Naqd al-adabi al-hadith* (Cairo, 1964): 438-442.

Isma'il, 'Izz al-Din. *Al-Shi'r al-'Arabi al-mu'asir* (Beirut, 1967): especially 73-76, 121-123, 341-342.

Jayyusi, Salma K. *Trends and Movements in Modern Arabic Poetry*, 2 Vols. (Leiden, 1977): especially Chapter 8.

Kamal al-Din, Jalil. *Al-Shi'r al-'Arabi al-hadith wa ruh al-'asr* (Beirut, 1964): 397-442.

Karam, Antun G. *Madkhal ila dirasat al-shi'r al-'Arabi al-hadith* (Beirut, 1967): 282-283.

Khazin, William and Ilyan, Nabih. *Kutub wa udaba'* (Sidon-Beirut, 1970): 61-70.

Mtanius, Michael. *Dirasat fi al-shi'r al-'Arabi al-hadith* (Sidon-Beirut, 1968): 37-63.

Muruwwa, Husayn. *Dirasa naqdiyya fi da'wa al-manhaj al-waqi'i* (Beirut, 1965): 374-419.

Al-Rayyes, Riyad N. *Al-Fatra al-harija* (Beirut, 1962): 16-168.

Razzuq, As'ad. *Al-Ustura fi al-shi'r al-hadith* (Beirut, 1959): 27-40.

Safadi, Muta'. Al-Thawri wa al-'Arabi al-thawri (Beirut, 1961): 325-341.

Al-Saharti, Mustafa A. *Al-Naqd al-adabi* (Cairo, 1962): 34-43.

Shukri, Ghali. *Shi'runa al-hadith ila ayn?* (Cairo, 1968): 72-73, 134-135, 145.

_____. *Al-Turath wa al-thawra* (Beirut, 1973): 241-242, 245-248.

B. Articles, reviews, and interviews

'Abd al-Sabur, Salah. "Naqd qasidat 'Al-Jisr,'" *Al-Adab* 6 (June 1957): 70.

Abu Dib, Kamal. "Fi al-sura al-shi'riyya," *Mawaqif* 27 (Spring 1974): 17-56.

Al-'Alim, Mahmud Amin. "Taqyim li 'adad al-shi'r al-khass," *Al-Adab* 5 (May 1966): 13-15, 76-78.

'Allush, Naji. "Muqabala Adabiyya," *Al-Adab* 8 (August 1965): 14-15.

Al-Amir, Daisy. "Khalil Hawi fi *Nahr al-ramad,*" *Al-Hikma* 6 (June 1959): 48.

_____. "Fi al-madaris al-adabiyya wa fi mafhum al-umma alladhi yanfi al-madaris," *Al-Nahar* (1 September 1957): 4.

Anonymous. "Hadith ma' Khalil Hawi hawl *Al-Nay wa al-rih* wa nahjuh al-shi'ri," *Al-Hikma* 2 (February 1961): 11.

Anonymous. "Mata Khalil Hawi," *Al-Safir* (7 June 1982): 13.

Anonymous. "Prix de la poésie: Khalil Hawi, 'La Flute et la Vent,' " *L'Orient Littéraire* 100 (December 1962): 5.

Anonymous. "Al-Prufissur Khalil Hawi li kursi Jiwit [Jewett] fi al-Jami'a al-Amrikiyya," *Al-Nahar* (17 February 1982): 7.

Anonymous. "Thalathat shu'ara' wa thalath mudun," *Al-Ahram* (29 June 1962): 13.

Al-Ansari, Muhammad J. "Min khilal qasidat 'Dabab wa buruq': nazarat fi shi'r Khalil Hawi," *Al-Adab* 5 (May 1972): 22-26.

_____. "Ru'ya Khalil Hawi 'Min Salih ila Thamud,' " *Al-Anwar* (21 February 1975): 12.

'Ataya, Raif. "Al-Hawi wa tajribat al-shi'r al-hadith," *Al-Adab* 4 (April 1962): 56-57.

_____. "Al-Inbi'ath wa al-thawra wa al-'awda fi qasidat Khalil Hawi, 'Risalat al-ghufran min Salih ila Thamud,' " *Qadaya 'Arabiyya* 1 (April 1975): 70.

_____. "Al-Naqd al-'aqa'idi," *Al-Adab* 9 (September 1961): 45.

'Awad, Rita. "An Interview," *Al-Hawadith* (6 April 1979): 63.

_____. "Al-Mawt wa al-inbi'ath fi shi'r Khalil Hawi," *Al-Adab* 1 (January 1974): 38-44.

'Awwad, Simun. "Al-Batunji al-ladhi asbah duktur," *Al-Mawasim* 5 (July 1966): 34-36.

Barakat, Halim. "*Nahr al-ramad,*" *Al-Nahar* (12 November 1957): 4.

Baydun, 'Afaf, "Khalil Hawi fi 'Wujuh al-Sindibad,' " *Al-Jarida* (8 May 1960): 7.

_____. "Khalil Hawi sha'ir taharrar min kull tahajjur wa istajab li al-ma'na al-tarikhi fi 'alam al-jamaliyyat," *Al-Hikma* 6 (June 1960): 19-21.

_____. "Ma' 'Al-Bahhar wa al-darwish,' " *Al-Jarida* 1086 (July 1956): 7.

_____. "*Nahr al-ramad:* ra'id al-ittijah al-wujudi," *Al-Adab* 5 (May 1958): 24-26.

_____. "*Al-Nay wa al-rih,*" *Al-Hikma* 6 (June 1961): 16.

_____. "Ra'i akhar fi Khalil Hawi," *Al-Hikma* 6 (June 1961): 16.

_____. "Al-Zawiya al-adabiyya," *Al-Jarida* (27 November 1960): 10.

Al-Braks, Ghazi. "*Nahr al-ramad:* tajriba fadhdha," *Al-Nahar* (9 January 1958): 4.

Bsat, Fawziyya. "Ma'al-sha'ir Khalil Hawi," *Durub* 24 (June 1965): 20-27.

Bukhti, Slayman. "Yamut al-sha'ir fa al-layl ghabat," *Al-Nahar* (12 June 1982): 7.

Fakhri, Majid. "*Nahr al-ramad* li Khalil Hawi [review], *Shi'r* 4 (Fall 1957): 93-96.

Freyz, Nuwar. "Muqabala ma'al-duktur Khalil Hawi," *Medicus* 2 (November 1965): 6-7.

Geha, George. "Khalil Hawi Sha'ir 'imlaq," *Al-Nahar* (5 July 1957): 4.

Ghanim, 'Abd Allah. "*Nahr al-ramad,*" *Al-Nahar* (10 November 1957): 4.

Ghanim, Robert. "Sab'at as'ila ma'Khalil Hawi: *Bayadir al-ju',*" *Al-Safa* (7 May 1965): 2.

Ghanimi, Muhammad H. "Al-Shi'r al-hadith," *Al-Majalla* (Cairo) 79 (October 1962): 124-125.

Ghassub, Yusif. "Naqd qasidat 'Al-Nay wa rih al-raml,' " *Al-Adab* 3 (March 1959): 69.

Ghurayyeb, Laure. "*Bayadir al-ju',*" *L'Orient* (18 April 1965): 4.

Haddad, Fuad S. "*Al-Nay wa al-rih* li Khalil Hawi," *Al-Adab* 7 (July 1961): 37-38.

Al-Hadidi, Dalal. "Kalima fi *Nahr al-ramad,*" *Al-Nahar* (17 December 1957): 4.

_____. "Sha'ir al-ramad," *Al-Nahar* (22-26 August 1957): 4, in all issues.

Hijazi, Abd al-Mu'ti. " 'Al-Majus fi Urubba': Khalil Hawi," *Al-Adab* 11 (November 1957): 81.

_____. "Al-Qasa'id," *Al-Adab* 6 (June 1960): 13, 70-74.

_____. "Naqd qasidat 'Al-Sindibad fi rihlatihi al-thamina,' " *Al-Adab* 6 (June 1960): 13, 70-73.

Al-Hilw, Ibrahim. "Qadiyyat al-shi'r al-hadith," *Al-Ahad* (15 May 1966): 34-35.

Haqqi, Yahya. "Harakat al-tajdid fi al-shi'r al-'Arabi al-hadith," *Al-Majalla* 144 (January 1968): 87-98.

Al-Hasan, Bilal. "Muqabala adabiyya ma' Khalil Hawi," *Al-Hurriyya* 264 (14 June 1965): 4.

Hawi, Iliyya. "Hawl 'Dabab wa buruq' li Khalil Hawi: al-shi'r wa al-sha'ir fi qasida," *Al-Adab* 6 (June 1972): 34-36.

_____. "Hawl 'Al-Dhura al-bayda','" *Al-Adab* 7 (July 1955): 67.

_____. "Al-Madmun al-wujudi fi *Nahr al-ramad*," *Al-Ma'arif* 5 (May 1961): 28-33.

_____. "Al-Madmun al-wujudi fi *Al-Nay wa al-rih*," *Al-Adab* 4 (April 1961): 18-22, 77-79.

_____. "Al-Sura bayn al-shi'r al-qadim wa al-shi'r al-mu'asir," *Al-Adab* 2 (February 1960): 53-57.

Haydar, Adnan. Review of *Gibran Kahlil Gibran: His Background, Character and Works*, by Khalil Hawi. *The Daily Star Supplement* (1 May 1972): 10.

Al-Haydari, Buland. "Al-Qasa'id: 'Dabab wa buruq' li Khalil Hawi," *Al-Adab* 4 (April 1972): 14.

Ibn Jallun, Al-Tahir "La Mort de Khalil Hawi," *Le Monde* (9 July 1982).

'Isa, Salah. "Al-Abhath," *Al-Adab* 2 (Feb. 1974): 12-13, 65-66.

Isma'il, Muhyi al-Din. "Ra'y fi al-shi'r al-'Arabi al-hadith," *Al-Adab* 5 (May 1964): 34-37.

Jabara, Wadi'a. " 'Al-Bahhar wa al-darwish' li Khalil Hawi," *Durub* 29 (February 1969): 35-36.

Jabr, Jamil. "*Gibran Kahlil Gibran* li Khalil Hawi" [review], *Hiwar* 5 (July-August 1963): 120-121.

_____. "Khalil Hawi fi *Nahr al-ramad*," *Al-Jarida* 1529 (15 December 1957): 7.

Al-Jabri, Muslim. "Fi al-shi'r: al-ma'rifa al-shi'riyya," *Al-Aqlam* (May 1978): 27.

Al-Jayyusi, Salma. 'Shi'r Khalil Hawi sawt jil bi akmalih," *Al-Adab* 4 (April 1958): 35-39.

_____. "Al-Shi'r al-'Arabi tatawwuruh wa mustaqbaluh," *'Alam al-fikr* 4:2 (July 1973): 49-53.

Al-Jisr, Basim. "Al-Shi'r al-hadith bayn al-shi'r wa al-la-shi'r," *Al-Usbu' al-'Arabi* 89 (February 1961): 10-11.

Al-Jundi, 'Ali. "*Nahr al-ramad*," *Al-Ahad* 518 (29 January 1961): 42.

_____. "Al-Shi'r fi Suriyya," *Al-Hikma* 5 (May 1963): 17-18.

_____. "Al-Shi'r wa al-sha'ir," *Al-Ma'arif* 5 (May 1962): 10-12.

Al-Jundi, In'am. "Adab," *Al-Usbu' al-'Arabi* 241 (1964): 63.

_____. "*Al-Nay wa al-rih* li Khalil Hawi," *Al-Usbu' al-'Arabi* 84 (January 1961): 9.

Jurdaq, Halim. "Min Halim Jurdaq ila Khalil Hawi," *Al-Nahar* 7486 (10 May 1960): 4.

Kanafani, Ghassan. "Qadiyyat al-shi'r fi hadith ma' Khalil Hawi," *Al-Ma'rifa* 5 (May 1962): 164-167.

Karam, Antun G. "*Gibran Kahlil Gibran* li Khalil Hawi," *Al-Abhath* 2 (February 1963): 268-271.

Al-Khal, Yusuf. "Hadhih al-qasida miftah thawra," *Al-Jarida* 1068 (24 June 1956): 7.

Khayr-Allah, As'ad. "An Interview," *Al-Hawadith* (28 July 1978): 54.

Al-Khazin, William. "Khalil Hawi 'alaqat hulwa wa afkar: rahat al-muntahir takhalusan min yas," *Al-Nahar* (10 June 1982): 13.

————, and Ilyan, Nabih. "Kitab wa adib," *Huna Bayrut* (June 1963): 41.

Al-Khuri, 'Abduh. "Al-Duktur Khalil Hawi wa hadith 'an al-shi'r al-hadith," *Al-Jumhur al-jadid* (10 June 1965): 50.

Khuri, Alfred. "Khalil Hawi wa al-tajdid," *Al-Jarida* 2510 (February 1961): 10.

Al-Khuri, 'Atif. "Hawl ma kutib 'an *Nahr al-ramad*," *Al-Adib* 4 (April 1958): 65-66.

Kilfat, Khalil. "Rihlat Khalil Hawi al-thalath," *Al-Adab* 3 (March 1966): 77-80.

Al-Kubissi, Tarrad. "I'adat taqyim mafhum al-hadatha fi al-shi'r," *Al-Fikr* (August 1969): 69.

————. "Al-Tadwir fi al-qasida al-haditha," *Al-Aqlam* (January 1978): 6.

Al-Maghut, Muhammad. "Khalil Hawi wa 'uqdat al-khusum," *Al-Ma'rifa* 8 (August 1962): 151-153.

Malhas, Thurayya. "Khalil Hawi, madha qulta 'ala al-tilifizyun?," *Al-Nahar* 9356 (5 June 1966): 16-17.

Al-Ma'luf, Emile. "Khalil Hawi sha'ir al-'asab al-mahmum," *Al-Jarida* 1545 (5 February 1958): 6-7.

————, and 'Ataya, Raif. "Rayan fi qasidat 'Al-Sindibad fi rihlatih al-thamina,'" *Al-Adab* 7 (July 1960): 26.

Ma'luf, Rafiq. "Ma' diwan *Nahr al-ramad*," *Al-Jarida* 1465 (2 October 1967): 2.

Mansur, Farid. "Khalil Hawi," *Al-Nahar* 15177 (12 January 1983): 13.

Mansur, Munaf. "Tajribat al-madina fi al-shi'r al-'Arabi al-mu'asir," *Al-Adab* 4 (April 1974): 42-47.

————. "Tajribat al-madina 'ind Khalil Hawi," *Qadaya 'Arabiyya* 5 (September 1974): 109-118.

Al-Muflih, Muhammad A. "Al-Thawra fi shi'r Khalil Hawi," *Al-'Amilun fi al-naft* 39 (May 1965): 38.

Muhammadiyya, Ahmad S. "Khalil Hawi wa 'uyubuh," *Al-Sayyad* (11 November 1965): 44-45.

Muhyi al-Din, Muhammad. "Naqd qasidat 'Al-Juruh al-sud,'"

Al-Adab 9 (September 1961): 72.

Muruwwa, Husayn. "Al-Qadim wa al-jadid wa ma huwa tabi'i fi al-adab," *Al-Mawqif al-Adabi* 5 & 6 (September-October 1971): 10-28.

Muyassar, Urkhan. "Naqd qasidat 'Da'wa qadima,' " *Al-Adab* 7 (July 1961): 67-68.

_____. "Naqd qasidat 'Li'azar: 1962,' " *Al-Adab* 7 (July 1962): 49-50.

Na'imy, Nadim. "*Al-Nay wa al-rih,*" *Al-Hikma* 6 (June 1961): 235-236.

Najm, Muhammad. "Hadith 'an al-shi'r al-hadith," *Al-Thawra al-'Arabiyya* (15 February 1965): 5.

Al-Naqqash, Raja. "*Al-Nay wa al-rih* akthar min muhawala," *Al-Anba'* 636 (8 August 1964): 7.

Nasr, Nasim. "Khalil Hawi ra'id wujudiyya," *Al-Adib* 5 (May 1961): 23-24.

_____. "*Nahr al-ramad* li Khalil Hawi," *Al-Adib* 2 (February 1958): 54-56.

Nimr, Nasib. "Hawi wa Mayakufski wa Vadiyiv: fa ya mawt zur, inna al-hayat dhamima," *Al-Nahar* (24 June 1982): 13.

Norin, Luc. "Présence de Khalil Hawi, ou le 'Full Life' existentiel," *La Revue du Liban* (2 April 1960): 32-33, 70.

Qabani, Nizar. " ' 'Awda ila Sadum,' " *Al-Adab* 10 (October 1957): 76-77.

Qatmeh, Khalid. "Madaris am dur hadana," *Al-Nahar* (7 September 1957): 4.

_____. " 'Nahr al-mawt,' " *Al-Nahar* (3 September 1957): 4.

Qubrusi, 'Abd Allah. "Kitab min 'Abd Allah Qubrusi ila Adunis, Hawi wa Idris," *Al-Nahar* (24 January 1980): 9.

_____. "La Sa'id Aql, la Adunis, la Khalil Hawi ashab madaris," *Al-Nahar* (18 August 1957): 4.

Al-Rahib, Hani. "Hiwar hawl *Bayadir al-ju',*" *Al-Adab* 8 (August 1965): 65-68.

Al-Rayyes, Najib R. "Hawi wa Adunis wa siwahuma," *Hiwar* 5 (August 1962): 147-154.

Rifqa, Fuad. "Khalil wa al-baruda: mubaraka al-ard al-aqdam," *Al-Nahar* (4 January 1981): 7.

Al-Rimawi, Mahmud. "Al-Duktur Khalil Hawi bashshar fi shi'rih bi al-hayat thumma intahar," *Al-'Arabi* 286 (September 1982): 29-32.

Sa'b, Adib. "Khalil Hawi: sha'ir la yamut," *Al-Mustaqbal* 284 (31 July 1982): 57.

Sa'b, Husayn A. "Hawl maqal 'min al-ma'sat ila al-malhama,' "

Al-Adab 10 (October 1961): 66.

Sab, Najib. "Al-Shakhs al-'asabi wa al-damir al-mustashrif,' *Al-Nahar* (9 June 1982): 13.

Al-Sabbah, Siham. *"Nahr al-ramad,"* *Al-Ma'arif* 2 (February 1962): 59-60.

Sa'd, 'Ali, "Naqd qasidat 'Jinniyyat al-shati,' " *Al-Adab* 8 (August 1961): 14, 57-59.

Sadiq, Habib. "Athar al-qadiyya al-Filistiniyya 'ala al-shi'r al-hadith fi Lubnan," *Al-Adab* 5 (May 1975): 101-102.

Safadi, Muta. *"Bayadir al-ju':* 'an al-mu'anat wa al-mas'uliyya," *Al-Adab* 7 (July 1965): 8-10, 60-66.

———. "Hawl shi'r Khalil Hawi," *Al-Adab* 3 (March 1961): 10-14, 70-73.

———. "Simfuniyyat *Al-Ra'd al-jarih,"* *Al-Thaqafa al-'Arabiyya* 14 (December 1974): 34-41.

Sa'id, 'Ali Ahmad. "Qadiyyat al-shi'r al-'Arabi al-hadith," *Afkar* 1 (January 1961): 122-125.

Sa'id, Hamid. "Nazarat fi al-shi'r al-hurr," *Al-Ma'arif* 8, 9 (August, September 1963): 76-84.

Al-Sakr, Hatim. "Qira'a fi nass shi'ri hadith: nashid 'al-Jisr,' *Nahr al-ramad,"* *Al-Tali'a al-Adabiyya* (July 1980): 26.

Al-Samirra'i, Majid S. *"Bayadir al-ju'* wa turbat al-tajarib," *Al-Ma'rifa* 61 (March 1967): 143-147.

Sardawi, Musa. "Hadith ma' al-duktur Khalil Hawi," *Al-Adab* 7 (July 1963): 72-73.

Sasin, Tawfiq. "Nizar wa Khalil," *Al-Nahar* (5 November 1967): 2.

Sayigh, Samira. "Ma' al-sha'ir Khalil Hawi," *Al-Usbu' al-'Arabi* 235 (9 January 1963): 70-74.

Sayigh, Tawfiq. "Al-Shi'r al-mu'asir taht mijhar sahib 'al-qasida K,' " *Al-Safa* (2 September 1962): 2.

Al-Sayyab, Badr. "Hadith 'an al-adab wa al-uduba'," *Al-Hawadith* (1 June 1962): 19.

Sayyid Ahl, Abd al-Aziz. "Naqd qasidat 'Al-Khudra al-tafiha',' " *Al-Adab* 4 (April 1954): 54.

Shalaq, Ali. "Fi majra *Nahr al-ramad,"* *Al-Nahar* (3 November 1957): 4.

———. *"Nahr al-ramad* 'asab jadhdhab," *Al-Nahar* (9 October 1957): 4.

Sharara, 'Abd al-Latif. "Naqd bahth min al-ma'sat ila al-malhama," *Al-Adab* 10 (October 1961): 10.

Sharara, Waddah. "Al-Sha'ir al-Lubnani khatimun hayatahu harakatan fi 'alam al-dalala," *Al-Nahar* (18 June 1982): 13.

Al-Shibani, Sa'id. "Hal li al-shi'r al-jadid falsafa?," *Al-Ma'arif* 5 (May 1962): 39-45.

Shukri, Ghali. "Ittijah al-sahm li harakat al-shi'r al-hadith," *Hiwar* 3 (March 1966): 58.

_____. "Qadaya al-adab wa al-udaba'," *Al-Adab* 1 (January 1963): 15.

Shurayh, Mahmud. "Arba'a sharaqu fi usturat al-mawt wa al-inbi'ath," *Al-Nahar* (13 July 1978): 9.

_____. "Munakh Khalil Hawi, mir'at ghaybiyya," *Al-Nahar* (16 July 1978): 10.

_____. "Tajribat al-madina fi shi'r Khalil Hawi," *Al-Fikr al-'Arabi al-mu'asir* 10 (February 1981): 89-97.

Swayd, Mahmud. "Madha wa limadha yaktub al-kuttab fi Lubnan?" *Al-Usbu' al-'Arabi* 369 (1966): 52-55.

Tarabishi, George. "Khalil Hawi bayna *Nahr al-ramad* wa *Al-Nay wa al-rih,*" *Al-Adab* 9 (September 1961): 14-16, 77-79.

_____. "Rudud thalatha," *Al-Adab* 11 (December 1961): 66-68.

Tumeh, Edward. "*Kahlil Gibran: His Background, Character and Works* by Khalil Hawi," *Middle East Forum* 39 (December 1963): 35.

Wazin, Abduh. "Khalil Hawi al-sha'ir tamaddad fa ishtadda 'alayh al-hisar," *Al-Nahar* (9 June 1982): 13.

Zaki, Ahmad K. "Hawl maqabala ma' Khalil Hawi," *Al-Adab* 9 (September 1965): 9.

_____. "Nahw idyulujiyya jadida 'ind Khalil Hawi," *Al-Fikr al-Mu'asir* 20 (October 1966): 72-80.

_____. "Naqd abhath Muta' Safadi," *Al-Adab* 8 (August 1965): 77-78.

_____. "Taqyim li 'adad al-shi'r al-khass," *Al-Adab* 5 (May 1966): 13-15, 76-78.

Zayid, Ali 'Ushri. "Anmat shakhsiyyat al-Sindibad fi al-shi'r al-mu'asir," *Al-Thaqafa al-'Arabiyya* (April 1974): 35-39.

_____. "Al-Sindibad bayn al-turath wa al-shi'r al-mu'asir," *Al-Thaqafa al-'Arabiyya* (February 1974): 63.

_____. "Wujuh turathiyya fi shi'rina al-mu'asir: wajh al-Sindibad fi shi'r Khalil Hawi," *Al-Shi'r* (July 1978): 58-66.

Zayn al-Din, Ahmad. "Gibran al-an 'abra dirasat Khalil Hawi: jadwa li al-naqid wa al-bahith thumma al-sha'ir," *Al-Nahar* (15 December 1982): 11.

Zghayb, Henri. "Intihar Khalil Hawi: al-mawt li al-marra al-akhira," *Al-Nahar al-'Arabi wa al-dawli* 268 (21-27 June 1982): 50-52.

III. Translations into English and French (in alphabetical order)

"A l'Age de Glace" ["'Asr al-jalid"] and "Dans l'obscurité des entrailles" ["Fi 'atamat al-rahim" from "Wujuh al-Sindibad"]. Translated by Luc Norin and Edouard Tarabay in *Anthologie de la littérature arabe contemporaine: la poésie* (Paris, 1967): 182-184.

"Bottomless Pit" ["Hufra bila qa'," from "Lazarus 1962"] and "The Cave" ["Al-Kahf"]. Translated by Adnan Haydar. *Voices* (1973): 84-88.

"The Bridge" ["Al-Jisr"]. Translated by Shafiq 'Ataya. *Cedar Wings* 56-58 (June-August 1966): 11-12.

"Departure" ["Firaq"] and extracts from "The Bridge" ["Al-Jisr"]. Translated by Shafiq Megally. *Journal of Arabic Literature* 7 (1976): 86-88.

"The Genie of the Beach" ["Jinniyyat al-shati"]." Translated by Michael Beard and Adnan Haydar. *Nimrod* 24:2 (Spring/Summer 1981): 101-103.

"The Mariner and the Dervish" ["Al-Bahhar wa al-darwish"]. Translated by Fuad Hadda. *Mid-East* (April 1967): 17-19.

"The Mariner and the Dervish" ["Al-Bahhar wa al-darwish"]. Translated by Munah Khuri and Hamid Algar. In *Anthology of Modern Arabic Poetry* (Berkeley, 1974): 60-65.

"The Sailor and the Dervish"]"Al-Bahhar wa al-darwish"] and "The Bridge" ["Al-Jisr"]. Translated by Issa Boullata. In *Modern Arab Poets 1950-1975* (Washington, D.C., 1976): 33-37.

Selections from *The Threshing Floors of Hunger*. Translated by Adnan Haydar. *A.U.B. Today* (Spring 1979): 6.

"Sodom" ["Sadum"]. Translated by Jabra Ibrahim Jabra. In "The Rebels, the Committed and the Others." Reprinted in *Critical Perspectives on Modern Arabic Literature*. Edited by Issa Boullata (Washington, D.C., 1980): 200-201.

The Wind and the Flute [*Al-Nay wa al-rih*]. Translated by Lewis Ware (Emeryville, California, forthcoming).

IV. Theses and Dissertations on Hawi

Abu Najm, George. "Tajrubat al-madina fi shi'r Khalil Hawi" (M.A. thesis, The Lebanese University, Beirut, 1978).

'Awad, Rita. "Usturat al-mawt wa al-inbi'ath fi al-shi'r al-'Arabi al-hadith" (M.A. thesis, American University of Beirut, 1974).

Haydar, Adnan, *"The Threshing Floors of Hunger:* Translation and Introduction" (M.A. thesis, American University of Beirut, 1969).

Nasr Allah, Musa Ilyas. "Mafhum al-inbi'ath al-hadari fi *Al-Nay wa al-rih"* (M.A. thesis, The Lebanese University, Beirut, 1972).

Rumayli, Rumayli. "Al-Madmun al-fikri li *Nahr al-ramad* wa ab'adih al-wujudiyyah wa al-qawmiyya" (M.A. thesis, The Lebanese University, Beirut, 1971).

Saba, Ruba. "La Mort et la résurrection de la civilisation arabe. Essai d'étude critique sur l'oeuvre de trois poètes arabes modernes: la mythologie et les symboles" (Ph.D. dissertation, The Sorbonne, Paris, 1973).